A Hiker's Guide to
Scrambling
Safely

Tom Morin

Rocky
Mountain Books
Calgary–Victoria–Vancouver

Rocky Mountain Books
#108, 17665-66A Avenue
Surrey, BC V3S 2A7
RMB www.rmbooks.com

Library and Archives Canada Cataloguing in Publication
Morin, Tom, 1965-
A hiker's guide to scrambling safely / Tom Morin.

Includes index. ISBN 1-894765-66-4

1. Alpine scrambling. 2. Alpine scrambling--Safety measures. I. Title.
GV200.195.M67 2005   796.522'3   C2005-904021-1

Edited by Alister Thomas
Book design by Tony Daffern
Cover design by Vangool Design + Typography
Front cover photo: Scramblers on a rock step on Nahahi Ridge,
    Canadian Rockies. Photo: Sonny Bou.
Back cover photo: An exposed traverse on Compression Ridge,
    Canadian Rockies. Photo: Andrew Nugara.
All interior photos provided by the author unless otherwise indicated.

Printed in Canada

Rocky Mountain Books acknowledges the financial support for its
publishing program from the Government of Canada through the Book
Publishing Industry Development Program (BPIDP).

Contents

After 50 Years Temple's Tourist Route Still has Teeth

On the 11th of July, 1955, a group of eleven boys aged 12 to 16 were alone on the normal route up Mount Temple, near Lake Louise. They were unprepared; some were wearing baseball cleats and there was only one ice axe among them.

It was late in the day. It was 24 °C and they were on a snow-covered, avalanche-prone slope. And the worst did happen; an avalanche swept ten of the eleven 200 metres down the mountain, smashing them into rocks along the way. Seven were killed in one of North America's worst mountaineering accidents.

Back in 1955, Mt. Temple didn't see a fraction of the summiteers that is does today. On a fine summer weekend day, it's common to have thirty or more people clustered on the summit!

It's surprising that there has only been three fatalities since 1955.

Perhaps there haven't been more fatalities on Mt. Temple because people are starting to understand that scrambling is serious business. Scrambling is an activity between hiking and rock climbing, and has become a popular form of mountain recreation.

The view from the top of Mount Temple is spectacular. It really is worth the effort. But if you're going to go-for-it, don't make the same mistakes that others have. Recognise when the conditions are safe, go with another scrambler, stay on the route and be fit enough to enjoy it. Before you go, take a scrambling skills course or join a local club that can provide some training. And last of all, don't forget your camera.

Acknowledgments

This book took much longer to write than I expected. In the midst of it I swore I'd never write another, but now that it's finished I can't wait to start the next one. I learned that getting published is a team sport. I'm used to teams of two: my climbing partner and me. However, the team required to bring an idea to publication is somewhat larger. I haven't even met all the players!

I didn't accumulate the library of photographs necessary to properly illustrate this book. The following kind people contributed from their personal collection: Bob Spirko, Andrew Nugara and Sonny Bou. I'd like to thank Dave Stephens for not only contributing photographs, but for maintaining a fantastic web site and for being an all-round nice guy.

Lisa Paulson, the Public Safety Manager for Waterton Lakes National Park, greatly contributed to the final outcome. Her comments on the draft were insightful and flush with professional rescue experience. I hope I adequately interpreted her comments: any inaccuracies or misguidance are completely my fault.

I'd like to thank the guides I've learned from, the great friends I've climbed and hiked with, and the best climbing partner in the world ... my wife, Joanna. Without Joanna's encouragement, proofreading and modelling, the book might never have been finished.

Thanks to the Edmonton Section of the Alpine Club of Canada for maintaining such a good accidents and safety-related website (alpineclub-edm. org/accidents/index.asp).

Finally, the greatest thanks goes to Tony Daffern and Rocky Mountain Books. I grew up reading books published and written by Tony and Gill Daffern. The Canadian climbing community truly owes them a debt of gratitude. I had a great time working with Tony ... and the best thing about Tony is that he'd have no idea why I'd say such a thing.

Introduction

Scrambling—unroped climbing over relatively easy mountain terrain—is one of the more dangerous forms of mountain recreation. Most scramblers are hikers and backpackers with the urge to stand on the tops of surrounding peaks.

The hazards encountered when a person progresses from nature walks to long day hikes can easily be managed by going with experienced friends, choosing well-travelled trails and never straying too far from civilization. However, the progression from hiking to scrambling is no small step. It's a leap that places the hiker in the realm of the mountaineer. You're not walking—you're climbing. There may be no trail to follow so you will need to find the route. Descent is more difficult and may be by a different route than the ascent. There is likely to be scree and boulder slopes to climb, rock bands to negotiate and even steep snow slopes to cross or descend. Falls of many metres are possible and the scrambler can be seriously injured or even killed.

It is difficult, however, for confident, self-reliant hikers and scramblers, like ourselves, to accept that a deadly scenario that takes someone else's life could also befall us. After all, most of us are fit, smart and adventurous. Aren't we the most suited to safely travel in the mountains? Well, yes. And if we keep exercising that big brain we'll understand that a hiker new to scrambling needs to learn a few new skills.

The goal of this book is to help scramblers recognize when they have crossed the line between strenuous hiking and scrambling, identify the potential hazards and indicate skills that require specific training rather than a trial-and-error approach to learning. In the case of the latter, errors are potentially serious, even life-threatening.

This book is not a how-to manual on how to routefind or how to use ropes correctly to safeguard your companions; there are many good texts on such subjects. It does emphasize, however, that books are no substitute for personal instruction by a certified guide or by scrambling with an experienced, well-led and organized group of scramblers.

While researching scrambling accidents for this book, I recognized two distinct categories: those scrambling accidents that befell hikers with skill, experience, training and vigilance similar to my own, and those accidents that were so predictable and preventable that I could not imagine myself ever being involved. Rightly or wrongly, I dismissed the latter as scenarios that only happened to the uninformed, unprepared and irresponsible; I'm pretty sure that these people wouldn't have purchased this book. This book is written for the rest of us who understand that while mountain travel carries risk, that risk can be managed.

I've included summaries of actual scrambling accidents throughout this book. I hope readers find these instructional rather than frightening. The information provided in this text will help you avoid a similar fate.

What is scrambling?

What is scrambling? When people say that they're going hiking, I picture them walking through a green, rolling, alpine meadow. I see them enjoying a tranquil day away from the office, each wearing a small daypack, comfortable, wrinkled clothing and a baseball cap. If they said they're going rock climbing, I'd imagine them harnessed, roped and gripped. I can see their face tensing as they hunt for a line up the next pitch. If I told you I was going scrambling tomorrow, what do you imagine I'd be doing? What landscape do you see me in? Can you imagine the type of terrain I should be climbing and the terrain I should avoid? You know, most people can answer the first two questions—right or wrong—but, can't answer the third.

If you need some help with the above questions, it's here! This section will consider several methods to define scrambling: by comparing hiking and scrambling hazards, using "accepted" rating systems and by examining individual skill and experience. Hopefully, after reading this chapter everyone's mental image of scrambling should share similar elements.

But one simple fact should be stated immediately: scrambling is a mountaineering skill. Furthermore, there are two broad definitions of scrambling: unroped movement over non-technical terrain as part of a "greater" climb (a greater climb being an alpine mixed, ice or rock climb), or as a pursuit in and of itself ("Yesterday, I went hiking. Tomorrow, I'm going scrambling".). This book approaches the subject of scrambling with the latter definition in mind.

Comparing the hazards of scrambling and hiking
Comparing hazards common to both scrambling and hiking helps us understand scrambling's increased risks. There are two classifications of hazards encountered in the mountains: objective hazards and subjective hazards. In this book there are sections devoted to each of these classifications, however, a quick definition is necessary at this point to aid in our understanding of the comparisons below. An objective hazard is something that is or happens regardless of whether you are present in the mountains. Examples of objective hazards are avalanches, rockfall, floods, lightning and snowstorms. The second type of hazard—subjective—is things you have control over. They may be managed with experience, exist only because of your state of mind or be of a magnitude that is fully controlled by your perception. Examples of subjective hazards are skill, experience, fear, imagination and judgment.

Hiking along a trail and scrambling up a route
Most hiking trails in North America were created by Aboriginal peoples and early European explorers. Life was more fragile back then so trails were normally routed to provide safe passage through a mountain range,

Scrambler moving through a chimney on Mount Alderson—hardly a hiking trail.
Photo: Dave Stephens.

travel between waterways or to provide access to lush valleys rich with game. Since the trails had to be safe to walk, possibly while carrying heavy loads, most trails did not have an excessive risk of rockfall, they normally didn't go straight up an avalanche gully and they typically didn't traverse high ledges so narrow that even a mountain goat would want a rope. All the things that hiking trials are not, scramble routes can be.

If you're hiking a well-established and marked trail, you should be able to turn 180 degrees at any time and follow the markers right back to the parking lot. Scrambling routes, on the other hand, may have little evidence of their utilization. In some instances, there are absolutely no observable signs that anyone has been up the mountain before. Getting "off-route" is a serious concern when scrambling. If you remain scrambling off-route, you could find yourself at the foot of a cliff. Worse yet, you might be descending off-route and unable to stop before you sail over a cliff to your unscheduled demise. Scrambling requires routefinding skills that are significantly in excess of those required for hiking.

The consequences of getting "off-route" can be deadly. *A young man died scrambling on Mt. Fairview in 1992 when he became disoriented on descent. Poor weather had set in and he proceeded to descend off the wrong side of the mountain. He died due to injuries sustained in falls over multiple cliffs.*

Commitment

Commitment is something that mountaineers talk about when they're describing a route. If you're hiking along a trail a few hours from your car and it starts to snow—and it snows every month of the year in the Canadian Rockies—you might decide to turn around, retreat to the car and come back when conditions are more agreeable. If you're halfway up a challenging scrambling route, however, you may not be able to safely retreat when the snow flies. You may also determine that ascent is safer than descent, given the particular change in weather. That's commitment. If the route can be characterized by a high level of commitment, it's not easy to go home when you're halfway up.

Falling is bad style

I've tripped over my two left feet when I've snagged a tree root that had sprouted across a hiking trail. I've slipped on a steep snow-covered hiking trail and used my crotch and a tree to arrest my descent. But I haven't fallen while scrambling—not yet. If I had, I probably would have been saved by my belayer or my helmet. If I wasn't on belay or properly equipped, my wife might be writing this book by herself and dedicating it to her late husband … or new boyfriend. Scrambling falls can kill you. Freak accidents aside, falls or trips while hiking along a trail might only scuff your knee and make your face red.

Scramblers require skills that hikers don't need

There are many books available that can help you become a more proficient hikers; they mention skills such as learning how to walk uphill efficiently, how to safely cross a stream or how to wear your pack so there is optimal balance of the load between your hips and shoulders. However, I've written this book because material devoted to scrambling skills is normally found in the introductory chapters of a mountaineering text and seldom read by hikers. Also, courses are available that are entirely focused on scrambling skills. However, these courses are normally provided by alpine clubs or commercial mountaineering schools—most hikers don't immediately think to seek out these institutions. If you're new to scrambling, this book is a good start.

Scrambling skills are quite specific and are usually focused around continuous unroped movement on rock, ice and snow. I know people who have taken scrambling courses after learning to rock-climb or ice-climb. You may need to learn how to use an ice axe to safely traverse a slope and arrest a fall. You may need to develop rope skills to help you and your partner up or down a tricky pitch. You may never tackle scramble routes that require all these skills, but at least make sure you have the skills you need for the route you plan to climb. Skills take time to learn and develop.

A climber suffered a broken ankle and several other injuries in 1987 when he slipped while learning to use his crampons. He was ascending a steep section of snow when he turned to ask his friend for instruction. This caused him to lose his balance and begin an accelerated slide down the slope. Because he didn't know how to self-arrest, his ice axe was torn from his grasp. He then tried to stop his fall by jamming his cramponed boot into the snow, which, of course, immediately broke his ankle.

You need an experienced climber's good judgment

Before we discuss rating systems, a critical subjective hazard needs to be emphasized: judgment. In particular, bad judgment. Your ability to exercise good judgment should increase with experience. In the beginning, however, judgment is a subjective hazard that you have to recognize and defer to safety at any doubt. If you're scrambling up a bald rocky peak at noon on a warm June day, for example, you may see some ominous looking clouds developing. If you are not able to interpret cloud formations to determine the probability of a thunderstorm developing into a severe lightning hazard, you should make your judgment call on the side of safety and abort the climb. As you build your skills and experience, you may be able to rely on your meteorological assessments—but not until then. Becoming stranded on a route that you don't have the skills to climb can also be attributed to poor judgment. Pushing past your limits of physical fitness to the point of dehydration and collapse is, again, the product of poor judgment. The consequences of all this poor judgment are more severe on scrambling routes than hiking trails.

Later, I'll go into greater detail on managing objective and subjective hazards encountered when scrambling.

Grading systems for scrambling

As you spend more time in the mountains, and meet some truly wonderful people and amazing climbers, you may feel the need to compare your accomplishments with those of others. It's only natural to try to understand where you might fit within a group. You'll hear climbers talk of their accomplishments in the common language of grading systems. Very few weekend sport climbers or climbing gym enthusiasts, however, understand where scrambling fits into the many recognized grading systems. In fact, even a hike in a gentle alpine meadow has a place in most alpine grading systems. With respect to scrambling, I've found the Yosemite Decimal System (YDS) provides the best grading criteria. The YDS utilizes five classes, 1 to 5, with YDS 1 being hiking and YDS 5 being climbing. The 5th class is further subdivided into grades between 5.2 and 5.14 by using digits after the decimal point with 5.9 easier than 5.12 (spoken as "five-twelve"). Less skilled climbers will climb from 5.2 to 5.6. Advanced climbers climb 5.10s. Then, there are the ones who laugh at Spiderman's weak climbing skills as they tackle 5.11 and up.

YDS Class	Description	Helmet	Rope
1	**Hiking** • Recognizable and marked trail • Use of hands not required	Not carried	Not carried
2	**Easy Scrambling** • May be hiking off-trail, bushwhacking, in mountainous region • Hands may occasionally be required for balance, whether grabbing handholds or arms out stretched for balance • Most experienced hikers are very comfortable	May be carried	Normally not required
3	**Intermediate Scrambling** • Frequent use of hands is required for balance • Hands frequently required for climbing • Multiple handholds and footholds are easily found by trained beginners • Belay may be required to provide comfort through more exposed sections • Pitches are seldom near vertical • Any vertical pitch will be short	Worn	Carried
4	**Difficult Scrambling** • Most climbers will want a belay for some pitches • Beginners would likely need to be guided up and belayed for safety and comfort • Handholds and footholds are not easily identified by trained beginners • Skills with movement on rock is required • Many pitches may be near vertical	Worn	Frequently used

tection	Routefinding	Commitment	Exposure	Comments
...\	Trail is marked	Turn around and walk out	Minimal	Rockfall and avalanche hazards normally do not exist when trails are in condition.
...rmally re-...red	Trail may not be marked but route is obvious. Typically called a Yak trail. Follow the tracks	Normally travel is easily reversed, but some caution is normally required while downclimbing	Minor exposure normally can be avoided	Severe fear of heights might cause some discomfort. Injuries from falls are likely minor. Most hikers in mountainous regions of North America have likely travelled 2nd-class terrain when on more rugged trails. Rockfall hazard would be minimal, but avalanche hazard may exist in early season.
...ural ...tection ...eadily ...ntified ...trained ...inners	Routes are normally easily found by trained beginners. Untrained beginners may find themselves off route, but normally without severe consequences.	A hazard must be understood and considered. Retreat may be difficult, time consuming or unsafe.	Injuries from falls are likely severe or fatal. Comfort with exposure is necessary.	Never confused with a hiking trail. Most hikers would not normally attempt these routes. Most trained beginners will find themselves comfortable on 3rd class terrain after a season of progressively more challenging scrambling. Rockfall and avalanche hazards must be managed.
...ural ...tec-...1 can ...found ...h ex-...ience	Routefinding skills may be critical to the success of the climb. Climbing off route could have severe or fatal consequences.	Significant	A fall would be fatal. Exposure may be severe throughout the route.	4th class terrain is the realm of the trained and experienced climber. Beginners would be very uncomfortable, even if well trained. These routes are admirable long-term objectives for beginners as long as appropriate experience and skill is gradually acquired.

A good example of 2nd-class terrain—basically a "yak trail."

3rd-class terrain. Note the absence of a trail. Photo: Dave Stephens.

While most climbing publications and park information centres will communicate climbing difficulty using the YDS, scrambling ratings are subjective and can change with time, as you'll see when we discuss scrambling guidebooks. The table on page 12 and 13 describes the characteristics of routes of classes YDS 1 to 4. Study this table. It's important for scramblers to understand where hiking stops and scrambling begins. Even more important is to understand where scrambling stops ... and real rock climbing begins.

In the case of YDS 5, the leader places protection using chocs, cams, bolts or pitons, helmets are worn and a rope is used. Leader skills are required and a leader fall can be serious if these skills are weak. Commitment depends on the route and the amount of protection available. This is not scrambling. If this is what you want to do, you've bought the wrong book.

It can be difficult, nonetheless, to distinguish between a 4th- and 5th-class route if you have no rock climbing experience and don't know how to lead and place protection. It's probably best to develop some rules of thumb (page 19) that help you determine if you're on a scrambling route or if you're venturing into 5th-class terrain. I have rules that I can use for any scramble. I don't employ them too often on 2nd- and 3rd-class routes, but they come in particularly handy when I find a route intimidating and I'm trying to decide if it's objectively dangerous, or if I'm just subjectively anxious. That's normally the more difficult 4th-class stuff.

Using skills and experience to define scrambling

We've looked at scrambling in terms of comparing it to hiking and where it fits in the popular Yosemite Decimal System. But what about a more subjective classification based on individual comfort? You may be able to scramble over a bit of rock, yet I might feel uncomfortable on the same rock if I were not protected. A 3 m- (10 ft-) high section of near vertical rock might be a scramble to some and a protected rock climb to others. Can we use these criteria to classify a route as a scramble or non-scramble? The short answer is: no. The long answer is: the more you climb, the more comfortable you'll become. I don't need a rope every place that I used to. There are routes, where I had always thought protection was required, that I now scoot up with ease. The most important point to remember is that I have changed ... but the rock has not. My comfort with risk has changed. The exposure (more on exposure later) has not. The same will happen to you.

When I describe a scramble route to someone, I understand that I'm describing something between hiking and technical rock climbing. I think that most people would not consider it a hike and most rock climbers would not be placing protection. Be that as it may, I really have no control over what the other person understands. Hopefully, they'll take the time to understand what they're getting into in the same way you and I have.

Mountaineering is characterized by freedom and personal responsibility. Only you can determine how you'll climb a route. If you choose a route

This easy pitch of rocking climbing would likely be rated at 5.2. Short, vertical pitches like this are often encountered on scrambling routes, but new scramblers beware: a fall from here could prove fatal. Photo: Dave Stephens.

Similar terrain to the photograph above, however, this climber knows he's leading an easy 5th-class route, and is leading on a rope. Photo: Dave Stephens.

and a method based on limited experience and bring fewer skills than the route requires, you are responsible for the consequences of failure, and any reward—or criticism—that might come with success.

Understanding risk

It's important to understand the different elements that make up all accidents. A slip on rock does not necessarily lead to injury or death. However, a slip on a highly exposed route leading to a fall where the scrambler is not roped, not belayed or not wearing a helmet, can result in injury or death. The slip on the rock is the cause. The lack of equipment, or knowledge of its use, are causal factors. Human interaction with one or more objective hazards present in the mountains (much more on objective hazards later) is the cause of accidents. This cannot be changed. People can slip. Rain and snowfall can impair travel. Lightning can strike people. The causal or contributing factors, however, are within the scramblers control. You can wear a helmet and climb roped. You can avoid, or prepare for, inclement weather. You can learn how to reduce the probability of being struck by lightning.

The root cause of an accident is the most important element of risk analysis to learn, because addressing the root causes of incidents is likely to prevent a reoccurrence. Root causes can be lack of experience, lack of training or bad luck. (Poor judgment is often cited as a root cause of mountaineering accidents, however, poor judgment should be considered a causal factor which can be prevented by increased experience or training.) Actual bad luck, ideally, is the only root cause that should remain after all objective hazards have been addressed—and bad luck doesn't show its face very often. It's difficult to imagine incidents where the root cause is bad luck; a hiker killed when hit on the head by the largest hailstone ever recorded in 100 years or the roof of a cavernous sinkhole collapsing and swallowing a hiker travelling on a slope that has never seen such erosion. Bad luck in the mountains, sometimes referred to as acts of God, can only be avoided by staying at home. The choice is yours.

Difficult and exposed scrambling on Mount Galwey. A experienced and confident scrambler mig̱
be at home here ... but so could a beginner with a rope and a solid belay. Photo: Dinah Kruze.

How to decide if you're scrambling

- You know you're scrambling when you use your hands. In reality, you may not even be touching the rock. Some 2nd-class routes are "walkable," but you may find yourself somewhat off balance and holding your arms outstretched. I call that "using your hands for balance." It still is a 2nd-class route, and may not appear terribly difficult or scary, but it fits the YDS definition of an "easy" scramble.

- If you fell and were arrested by a belayer, would your weight be mostly on the rope alone? If yes, then you're not scrambling; you're climbing 5th class. A rope, on a scramble, should stop you from falling. After your fall is arrested, you should be able to stand up if not injured and start climbing again. No dangling!

- If the route is significantly exposed, can natural protection be easily identified and employed effectively? If natural protection might be ineffective, it's 5th class.

- Is any part of the route vertical, or very near vertical, for more than 3 m (10 ft) without effective natural protection available? If yes, a leader fall could be disastrous.

- Could you or your companions downclimb the route comfortably without a belay? If one of you can, then the other(s) may be belayed down. If no one can downclimb it, how do you ever expect to get home?

In case there is still some ambiguity surrounding the definition of scrambling, here's a list of what scrambling is NOT:

- Scrambling is NOT unroped climbing pitches of vertical rock longer than 3 m (10 ft). This is called 5th-class soloing.

- Scrambling is NOT climbing steep, ice-covered slopes. Scramblers need to cross small sections of ice, but climbing an entire ice slope requires skills and knowledge beyond that of scrambling.

- Scrambling is NOT climbing snow-covered slopes. See the reason above and substitute "snow" for "ice."

- Scrambling is NOT crossing glaciated terrain. Glaciers mean crevasses, and crossing glaciers requires specific training.

- Scrambling does not involve the placing of ice screws, snow pickets, pitons or other rock protection. Scramblers may employ "natural" protection, such as slings around horns (more on this later), but placing the "artificial" protection listed above requires additional training.

Guidebooks

I've never written a guidebook, so I now understand the incredible effort required. Among climbing guides, I believe Alan Kane has written one of the better ones. In the latest edition of *Scrambles in the Canadian Rockies*, Kane describes over 180 routes up 156 peaks. Alan, however, had climbed over 400 peaks as of 2003 when I began writing this book. The passion and commitment required to reach that many summits, and document the accomplishments, is beyond comprehension. I am appreciative of the introduction and access to mountains that guidebook authors have provided.

Readers should further appreciate the skill and experience these authors have accumulated, and the good judgment they have learned by managing the inevitable crises that have arisen. Although these are the attributes of a competent mountaineer, they also form the foundation for any bias and opinions inherent in their writing. All guidebooks, no matter how much the author focuses on purely technical detail, convey subjective opinions on climbing style and personal philosophy toward objective and subjective hazards. I encourage you to read the entire guidebook with a mind tuned to identifying inconsistencies or omissions that prompt you to seek additional information. It will assist you in choosing the climbs commensurate with your level of experience and training.

Those extra pages at the front of the book

In the preface of *Scrambling in the Canadian Rockies*, Kane notes a disturbing trend: "Although I suggested that readers follow a cautious progression, many folks start out with limited experience, yet see no need for instruction. Casual conversations have revealed that many skipped reading the introduction, the ratings' explanation and the hazard section. I find this a bit worrisome."

In the introductions, forewords and preparatory chapters of most guidebooks, the authors explain their intentions and assumptions. Many people don't appreciate the effort that guidebook writers put into these sections. Authors often include some of their most exciting experiences and present their philosophies. It can be the most critical section of the book.

I can't think of any of mountain guidebook author who would be persuaded by his editor or publisher to write some extra stuff and stick it at the front of the book because they needed to make it a little thicker. I know that most of us would much rather be climbing, or perhaps at the business end of a dentist's drill, than writing. The preparatory sections of a mountain guidebook may contain some information and suggestions that you already know. Read them anyway. Every few years a new edition of *Mountaineering The Freedom of the Hills* is printed. I reread the entire book, including the chapters that change little from edition to edition.

Scrambling is a skill. It is a combination of natural movement in unnatural locations (I say "unnatural locations" because there are normally no other reasons than a great view, exercise and psychological challenge to justify most scrambling—after all, there's no food, shelter or sane mate to be found en route). You should periodically refresh your knowledge and understanding—especially if your brain has spent the entire winter being stressed only by the pushing and shoving in the lineup for the chairlift. Information regarding the natural history of the area, tips on gear and clothing, notes about the weather and climate, permit requirements and suggestions about where to find additional information are critical to anyone new to an area. Colorado's weather and geology are unique when compared to the Pacific Northwest. A skilled and experienced mountain traveller wants to understand these differences. Remember that the author is not about to restate the relevance of every comment regarding risks and hazards in each individual route description. However, it's likely somewhere in the book, and normally well-identified at the front. Detailed subjects condensed into a concise format relevant to the geographical area covered by the book—now, that's worth thirty minutes of reading!

An author's rating system
Aside from the topics listed above, there is one key item that readers should try to understand when thumbing through a new guidebook: how has the author's level of mountaineering training, skill and experience influenced his difficulty rating of each route? Look for clues when you begin reading. Has the author taken extensive training over the years? Does the author now spend the majority of his time doing high-altitude mixed alpine routes? Perhaps that author started out scrambling, like you are, but may not remember the stomach butterflies that can appear on a high and exposed ridge.

You need to get a feel for the author's views on route difficulty. There will be a section—and the level of detail varies greatly—on the rating system employed. Hiking and scrambling guides tend to stray from accepted alpine rating systems because these systems provide descriptions of limited detail on the lower levels of difficulty. For example, the Yosemite Decimal System has increments for 5th-class climbs and provides clear criteria for each level, but treats 1st-, 2nd-, 3rd- and 4th-class routes as mere footnotes. The author could use an Easy, Moderate and Difficult rating system based either on the hardest move encountered, the time required to complete the climb or, possibly, the level of physical exertion encountered.

Once you fully understand the logic behind each rating, any inconsistencies in the individual route descriptions can be identified. Then, determine if a particular route has been rated conservatively or somewhat daringly. Inconsistencies in rating happen all the time, particularly in hiking and scrambling guides. Why? The rating of a scramble is normally developed based on objective hazards encountered en route, likely on the author's first attempt. The author is trying to make notes, mental or otherwise, on where to turn off the main trail, which gully to go up, along with mentioning any prominent peaks observable along the way and any hazards encountered. Some hazards are easier for the author to notice. And something that you feel should have been noted, the author may think otherwise. Where you might feel incredibly exposed at some point or feel that a section of rock should be at least protected by a belay, the author might have been able to carry on up without a second thought or extra bead of sweat. Remember, the author likely has more skill and experience than you and, therefore, manages objective hazards with more ease having minimized his subjective hazards over time. It's critical to remember that the rating only applies for certain conditions. Snow, rain and ice can transform an "easy" scramble into a deathtrap.

Forming part of the author's intended audience, with respect to climbing experience and skill, will determine how much you are able to benefit from the book. The author, however, may not have explicitly identified his audience. The first clue is any confusing jargon. If you don't understand what an "arête" or "couloir" is, more mountaineering training is required, not highschool French. If you're asked to place a "nut" or "Friend" in a crack, don't look to your climbing companions for a volunteer—you need some rock training.

I remember one scramble on a crowded peak in Canada's Banff National Park. It was a brutal slog up steep and unstable scree. Routefinding skills were necessary and the group coming up behind us had wandered hopelessly off-route. My partner and I watched them grunt up the final slope before the col, where we were resting and having a snack. As we finished our sandwiches, the group settled onto this tiny oasis of level ground. Immediately a debate erupted challenging the rating of the climb published in the current guide. They were sure the author had made a mistake by rating it a Moderate instead of a Difficult. They had traversed horribly exposed cliff bands and did not see a marker, cairn or compassionate soul anywhere along the route. They found the route exposed, longer and more physically demanding than expected. For some members of this group, it was their first outing in the Canadian Rockies. For others, their first scramble! As my partner and I inched our way toward the summit, we encountered a few tricky spots and began to discuss how the route was a little tougher than we, too, had expected.

While relaxing over a beer that night, I reread the route description and the author's explanation of the rating system. The time required to complete the route, elevation gain, maximum elevation and a reasonable route description were all in the book. The correlation between the author's explanation of Moderate and the route were flawless. We agreed with the author and concluded that the group must have only been interested in the route drawn on a photograph of the peak, read the rating and set out. Yes, it was steep, and yes, it was tough, but it did add up to a Moderate. If the members of the off-route group had spent more time in the local backcountry, they might have also agreed with the rating. And I'm sure the author did not expect that peak to be someone's first scramble.

What else is important in the book
Did the author climb every route? Some guidebooks are a compilation of route description from parties other than the author. Even though it is likely that the author climbed some, if not most, of the routes, the other descriptions could have been provided by the author's friends or acquaintances. This fact does not detract from the accuracy of the information, but it does indicate that any additional information may have to be sourced from someone other than the author.

The time to complete the route may be given in ascent time or round trip time. Note whether or not the author has included any time spent on a long approach hike; a backcountry scramble may begin from a remote hike-in campsite some distance from the parking lot. It's a good idea to determine your average walking speed on various terrains. The fastest I normally go with a heavy pack on flat trails is 4 km an hour (2.5 mi/hr). That slows down as the terrain becomes steeper.

Elevation gain is important. Most fit people can easily accomplish 300 m (1,000 ft) per hour. If you're really fit, and only carrying a small day pack, 450 m (1,500 ft) per hour is not uncommon. I bet the author of the guide-

Guide books can help get you to the summit, but a little homework on your part can go a long way. Photo: Andrew Nugara.

23

book is pretty fit. Since most scrambles are one-day affairs, the maximum elevation of a peak is not normally an issue in the U.S. lower forty-eight and most of Canada, where peaks rarely rise above 4,300 m (14,000 ft). It's unlikely that the average scrambler can gain enough altitude in one day to suffer any significantly adverse effects. But it is possible to experience some less serious effects of an oxygen deficient environment on a one-day scramble. An elevation gain of 1500 m (5,000 ft) may leave you puffing and humble. This relatively small change in elevation, however, can have some serious adverse effects if you attempt a summit immediately after travelling from an elevation that is lower than the starting elevation of the climb. This is a frequent occurrence in my neck of the woods. Tourists arrive from sea level to our mountain national parks at 1500 m (5,000 ft), then immediately decide to climb a 3000 m (10,000 ft) peak. Altitude sickness, or AMS (Acute Mountain Sickness), has been recorded in these instances.

Route directions are another detail that have to be understood. Chic Scott, the author of several guidebooks and *Pushing the Limits: The Story of Canadian Mountaineering*, went the extra mile to communicate this to his readers (it's at the front of the book, too!). Normally, if the author says to turn right at the big boulder on your approach to the peak, it's pretty obvious. However, some instructions may be less clear, such as, "look on the right side of the creek." The right side of the creek might refer to the direction of flow of the creek. Therefore, if you were standing in the middle of the creek facing downstream, the right side is your right-hand side. Hopefully, the author supplements these instructions with compass directions: north, south, east, west.

Selecting scrambles from a guidebook
It would seem obvious to start with a lower-rated scramble, then gradually attempt the more difficult—and that's the advice I'd give to hikers new to scrambling. As I climb more difficult routes, however, I have been taught humbling lessons when assuming that because I climbed one route the author rated as Difficult, I should have no problem climbing any of the other Difficult routes. Not so. Obviously, some Difficult routes are more difficult than others.

A scrambler's goals should include developing an intuitive assessment of objective hazards found in his local climbing area. This, and other skills acquired over time, can also make scrambling holidays safer and more enjoyable. If you're already scrambling at an advanced level in Washington's Cascades and desire a suitable challenge on a vacation to the Canadian Rockies, your skills and experience will serve you well, but some additional preparation is required. Ensure that you research and understand any objective hazards that are different or more severe than you're used to. Try to find guidebooks written by locals. Your odds of finding the most accurate information increase when you plan with the assistance of someone who's spent every weekend of his adult life in the local hills. And, for any guidebook, the more current the better—that lonely stretch of gravel road is now paved and lined with cottages, and a golf course has been imposed where a friendly trail once wiggled its way through mossy meadows. Approaches are subject to the most change. Keep current.

Beyond the guidebook

Experienced backcountry travellers know better than to put all their eggs in one basket. Before they embark on a challenging trip, they will gather as much information as necessary to guide them safely. How much information you'll need is largely linked to risk. For an easy scramble on one of those perfect summer days, your guidebook, hiking experience, hiking gear and enough sense to respect Mother Nature and her rocks should be sufficient. But for an early-season scramble from a remote backcountry campsite, where traversing steep snow and the use a rope and natural protection will be required, the planning may approach that of a small expedition, or at least, a serious alpine climb. Even if you're not ready to commit to such an endeavour, it's prudent to understand the sources of information available to support, or challenge, the guidebook.

The ability to use topographical maps is a must. If another guidebook has a reasonably good reputation, it's likely worth your time, especially for cross-checking ratings. Buyers beware, however. There are some lazy opportunistic buggers out there who blatantly plagiarize the guidebooks of others and offer nothing new in their own. Normally, only one favourite guidebook is recommended locally, and subsequent books fall short. However, supplementing a scrambling guide with the local hiking guide can get you from the trailhead to the base of the route much faster. Assorted photographs of the peak are helpful. If you're driving by the peak prior to your outing, snap a few with a digital camera and discuss them with someone who can explain the best route.

Value first-hand information. If you plan to scramble in or near a park, make sure you include a trip to the park information centre. Park wardens provide these centres with current trail and route conditions and any closure information. If you find that the information provided is incomplete, do not hesitate to contact the park's public safety office. While the wardens are always busy, they will return phone calls. Their job is to prevent accidents. They can provide detailed information on where scramblers commonly go off-route, whether any trail markers are missing or where the guidebooks may be less than accurate. Make sure you have exhausted all other sources first. Ask employees of gear shops if they do any local scrambling. If they're genuinely enthusiastic about scrambling, their information is likely good stuff. Local climbing clubs may regularly lead scrambles for novice and experienced climbers. Even if you're not a member, or just prefer a smaller group, call and ask to be referred to someone who's familiar with the route.

Finally, the Internet holds great potential, but use your judgment when surfing descriptions and opinions found in an on-line climbing log. The author may be less adept than the riveting prose implies. He may be the next statistic, or may have already contributed to a wealth of climbing accident knowledge.

Obviously, guidebooks are not climbing textbooks, nor do they hasten the improvement of judgment. No guidebook can substantially supplement sound training and experience. Recognize, however, the true merit of what all that "binding thickener" holds. Besides, we starving writers need our egos boosted. If someone says to me, without asking for his money back, "I read your book cover-to-cover," I'll feel a foot taller.

Accident scenario

A group of eight close friends gathered at a local trailhead at sunrise only to see that the hiking trail was closed due to the risk of wildfires in the area. Still wanting to make the most of the good weather, the group drove an hour farther down the highway to another trailhead that led to a popular scrambling route up one of the highest mountains in the area. The "leader" of the group reassured a few of the reluctant scramblers that a scramble was, more or less, just a steep hike and that the group had all the skill and fitness to be successful. No one had a helmet.

After an hour on the approach trail, the group was ascending the lower scree slopes of the peak. It was now mid-morning and there were many parties above them. They could hear shouts of "Rock!" coming from the parties above, but couldn't see or hear any subsequent rockfall. As they traversed below a steep face, one member of the group was struck by a football-sized rock and killed.

Injuries: no one else was injured.

What can we learn from this?
- Scramblers and climbers have been killed by rockfall—even when wearing a helmet.
- A helmet may have saved this life.
- It is critical to understand which terrain and which conditions can precipitate rockfall.
- This route is known for its scrambler-initiated rockfall: it's locally referred to as the "Bowling for People" route. Getting a late start on a route like this puts your party at greater risk.

Objective hazards

Objective hazards are hazards that exist regardless of our presence in the mountains. They include weather, avalanche, rockfall, fast or high water, wildfire, steep snow and ice, altitude and, to some degree, exposure and remoteness. The fact that weather changes and can become life-threatening is understood by most mountain travellers. But exposure may not be understood as an objective hazard. The objective nature of exposure and remoteness need to be fully understood before they can be managed.

The magnitude of individual hazards vary from region to region. You need to become familiar with your local climbing environment and understand the relative magnitude of objective hazards specific to that environment. In the Canadian Rockies, for example, rockfall is a significant objective hazard. On the other hand, you may be scrambling in a desert region of Southern California where flash floods may be the most severe objective hazard to consider.

An assessment of the objective hazards will determine whether the route is "in" or "out" of condition. Alpine climbing and scrambling routes are best climbed when the objective hazards are least severe and least likely to place the party in peril—the route would then be "in condition." (For example, a specific route may be best climbed in August, perhaps the driest season, and between 3 am and 1 pm—as the rockfall hazard would be minimized because ice is still bonding the loose rocks.)

Not only is it important to understand when an objective hazard is at its most severe and dangerous, but it's critical to understand that objective hazards can never be removed, solved, reduced or changed in any way. Therefore, objective hazards are only managed by avoiding them or doing something to minimize the effects of exposure to the hazards.

This key concept merits restatement: you need to avoid the hazard or minimize its adverse effects. You have no other options. An apprenticeship in mountaineering demands that you modify your behaviour and actions in response to risk analysis, and continuously seek to increase your mountain skills and knowledge—the more you learn and train, the better you'll be able to manage the hazards.

Mental checklist

Before we examine some objective hazards of particular relevance to scrambling, I'd like to propose a "mental checklist." Its purpose is simple: to alert the scrambler to a potentially dangerous situation with the intent of prompting a kind of "Go/No-Go" decision.

Analysis of mountaineering accidents reveal that misfortune tends to raise its head soon after some transition or change has occurred. Events that can precede an accident include: starting to climb after a break or discussion, a change in terrain or gear, a change in the weather or route

Mental checklist

Questions to ask yourself	
Are you having fun, free of fear and anxiety, and do you feel safe?	
If you get injured or need assistance, are you confident that the other members of your party will be able to help you?	
Is the route "in condition"? Do you have an alternative for the day if it isn't?	
Is there anything about this route that is new or more difficult than your previous scrambles? Is there a good turn-around point or do you have to complete the ascent and descend another way?	
How would you rate this scramble using the YDS?	
Do you have the gear and clothing you need?	
Is the route free of snow or ice?	

If you've answered "No" or you are unsure then ...
• Objective hazards need to be discussed—start talking about it • Think of subjective hazards: do you have the skill and experience needed for the route • Maybe you are uncomfortable with a decision regarding the route or hazards • Still can't figure it out? Then you've likely answered "No" to another question ...
• You better be able to take care of yourself because you're soloing, even though you are in a group • Members of a scrambling party should be able to help one another in an emergency situation • If you're leading complete novices on a scramble, you should have the skills and experience of a certified guide
• Remember that guidebook ratings are based on the route being snow-free and dry. The route may be "easy" or "moderate" when it's "in condition", but it could be an epic nightmare otherwise • You can change routes or temper your aspirations for the current route
• There is nothing wrong with scrambling near your limits, that's how we build skills, but if you're relying on a friend or a trip leader to get you through the crux, then you are responsible for any adverse consequences—not the "helper." If you're not comfortable with this, tone down your ambition or abort the climb.
Refer to the table on pages 12 and 13, but basically: • 2nd class – rough hike; • 3rd class – using hands with exposure, a fall will break bones; • 4th class – Huge exposure, fatal falls, tough routefinding; • 5th class – I thought you were scrambling?
• Climbers and scramblers carry and wear helmets. If you climb without a helmet, don't fall and pray that nothing falls on you • If the route is 4th class, you may want a rope for the more exposed or tricky sections • You should have packed the minimum clothing to survive any expected weather, plus a bivy sac, map and compass
• Snow can mean avalanche. Check the local avalanche safety office • If there is a significant amount of snow, do you have the skills to cross it safely? Do you need an ice axe and crampons? • If a fall would result in an accelerating slide, have you assessed the run-out?

Questions to ask yourself	
Did you check the most current weather report?	
Have you told a responsible person where you're going and when you expect to be back?	

condition, or the transition from belayer to climber—you get the idea. I sometimes find myself with an uneasy feeling and not knowing why I'm feeling that way. The Mental Checklist starting on the previous page helps me figure out whether I've missed a hazard and my subconscious is trying to get my attention. Whenever you feel a transition or change has occurred, and whenever you feel nervous, ask yourself these questions.

Exposure

"That route's pretty exposed." I've heard and said this phrase numerous times. This concept of exposure can be defined as the likely severity of an injury resulting from an unroped fall. The elements that determine the severity of injury are present regardless of our presence in the mountains: elements such as the length or distance of the potential fall, the angle of the slope, the nature of the rock, smooth slabs, etc.

Comfort with exposure takes time. Every time I climb Mt. Lady Macdonald near Canmore, Alberta, I start out convinced that I will not want a rope for the final crux ridge. And every time I get to that crux, even after seeing others stroll across it unroped, I still want the rope. It drives me nuts! I've climbed terrain that's considerably more exposed and could kill me ten times over, compared to Lady Macdonald. However, there's just something about that ridge that I can't get used to. I make no apologies and bear no shame.

If you've answered "No" or you are unsure then ...
• If you find yourself fully committed to the route when bad weather hits, you may not be able to safely retreat • You should know what weather to expect and be prepared to adjust your objectives or retreat in the face of unacceptable weather
• You need to tell someone where you're going; where you will be parked; your license plate number; make and model of your car; when you expect to be back; how long to wait before they report you as overdue; who to report to • If you have registered at the trailhead or park office, remember to register-out immediately after you are finished the climb • If you plan to use a radio, cellular or satellite phone to call for rescue, tell everyone in the party that you have the communications equipment and how to operate it (including what number to call) Never rely on these devices and always try to self-rescue first if it's safe to do so without risking further injury to yourself or other members of your party.

As with all objective hazards you need to avoid the hazard or minimize its adverse effects—remember that objective hazards can never be removed, solved, reduced or changed.

In order to recognize when a pitch is exposed, the scrambler needs to imagine the consequences of an unroped fall. This is difficult for many people in two ways:

• New scramblers may not have witnessed or heard of many climbing accidents, causing their imagined consequences to be eitjer exaggerated or minimized.
• Uncontrolled fear shaped by the imagination of horrific injury can paralyze a scrambler, which can result in a stranded scrambler.

As an aid to determining exposure, review the table on the YDS and the comments pertaining to 2nd-, 3rd- and 4th-class routes, then reread the section called "How to tell if you're scrambling." If a roped fall would leave you dangling in space, then you're rock climbing, not scrambling. If you wouldn't be left dangling, what about an unroped fall? Would you carry on sliding down the slope without much hope of slowing down or stopping? Or is any fall likely to be the equivalent to a fall on the sidewalk on your way to work? People trip over their own feet every day. Most live and laugh it off. If you imagine an unroped fall to result in serious injury due to the exposed nature of that section of the route, then you must take steps to minimize the adverse affects of that fall.

Exposure

- Continually assess the exposure as you climb
- Read about scrambling accidents in order to help you assess hazards
- Don't become paralyzed by your imagination
- You may have to find an alternate route or abort the climb if you do not have the skills and equipment to protect the route
- If you want a rope, take it. If someone asks for a rope, give it.
- With experience and training you will be able to safely climb more routes, but the exposure (objective) will not go away

Your first option is always to abort the route and find a less exposed one, or just leave. If there are no other suitable routes, and you're not going home, then you need to protect the route. Protecting 3rd- or 4th-class routes requires rope and belay skills as a minimum. The chapter on skills and training will guide you. For now, understand this: you have determined that the exposure is real and a fall could be disastrous. Continuing unroped in spite of that assessment is a decision that you alone must make and are completely responsible for. Feeling like you need a rope is subjective; more experienced climbers may or may not feel they need a rope on that particular pitch. If they decide to rope-up, they will likely have the skills to do so competently and confidently. Don't assume that just because you may be new to scrambling that others would simply stroll up the route. Your assessment of the pitch could be dead on. Finally, you do not have the right to cajole someone into climbing something that they are uncomfortable ascending, deny someone a rope or even jokingly rebuke them. Every scrambler has the right to a belay.

Scrambling is serious business and everyone's concerns must be respected. Learning to stick together and communicate is key.

A group of scramblers had a disagreement regarding the best descent route off a popular peak in 2001. One member of the group was determined to descend via a different route than the group had ascended. He struck out on his own while the rest returned via their previous route. The lone climber was overdue and the group reported him to local rescue personnel. He eventually found his way down, but he said he had to return to the summit and then descend the normal route. He discovered that the route he initially wanted to descend had several dangerous cliff bands.

Rockfall

Wear a climbing helmet on steep, unstable or rockfall-prone terrain. Climbing helmets save lives. Wear a helmet.

A climber was killed when he slid from a snow slope into a rocky gully in 1999. He sustained trauma to his head and several lacerations. He was not wearing a helmet. Investigators agree that the outcome may have been different had he been wearing a helmet.

All mountains erode, but the composition of the rock will determine the rate of erosion. The limestone of the Canadian Rockies, affectionately referred to as the "Rotten Rockies," erodes in a manner that creates a dangerous objective hazard called rockfall. Stating the obvious, a route is said to have a rockfall hazard if it's likely that rock will fall and could injure or kill climbers. In reality, the majority of scrambling and traditional rock-climbing routes have a rockfall hazard. In alpine climbing, however, rockfall may not be an issue on a glacier-walkup if the route never travels beneath, or close enough to, a rock face and stays out of the fall-line (more on the fall-line below). Scramblers and their gear also knock rock loose, although good climbers watch their feet and knock very few rocks loose. Test your hand- and foot-holds to ensure they are stable. On busy routes your greatest objective hazard can be other climbers and the rocks they send down on you.

In colder climates, it's the freeze/thaw cycle that is mostly responsible for the rockfall hazard. This could be a winter/spring, summer/autumn, sunny/cloudy or night/day (diurnal) cycle. A swing in temperatures can melt the ice that bonds the rock, or can weaken the structure by expanding ice as the day's melt freezes once again. Both these scenarios can result in rockfall. In warmer climates, where ice cannot form, rockfall is generally an erosive process accelerated by wind and by water from rain, swollen streams, etc.

It's easy to assess the rockfall hazard on routes that travel beneath steep, crumbled slopes. However, experience teaches climbers that the risk of rockfall needs to be assessed on every route. In the early 1990s, I was hiking to Wenkchemna Pass in Banff National Park. My peripheral vision captured movement on the slope to my upper right. About 700 m (2,300 ft) away, a rock the size of a house broke away from a pinnacle and crashed to a snow-covered ledge above me. The snow spit up as if it came from a water fountain at a Las Vegas hotel. I never heard a sound. I was travelling on a popular hiking trail with a turquoise alpine lake on my left and a grassy meadow to my immediate right: the thought of a rockfall hazard, therefore, had never entered my mind. I've included this example only to illustrate the temporary nature of mountains. Since this was not typical rockfall-prone terrain, if the boulder had rolled down the slope and crushed me, the accident would have likely been attributed to an act of God or just bad luck. The only way to avoid acts of God, or bad luck in the mountains is to stay

Typical Rockies rubble. Loose rocks can tumble down slopes and ruin your day. Note the helmet.

home. Since that is not an option for us, it's more constructive to discuss the rockfall hazard that we can manage.

Many scrambling routes wind their way up gullies or couloirs. These are dangerous bowling alleys where falling rocks can take some unexpected, gymnastic bounces.

Although it's not always possible, try to stay out of the fall-line when climbing up gullies (the fall-line is the direct downward path that a falling object would take if that path were influenced by gravity alone, and not any redirection due to hitting the slope). If the gully centre is the only line that provides any decent purchase for hands and feet, you'll need to determine which is the greater risk: sticking with the centre and accepting greater exposure to rockfall or trying to find a route up the side of the gully and accepting the consequences of a more difficult, and likely longer, climb. Remember that the quicker you climb through this hazardous section of the route, the less time you will be exposed to the hazard—it's not an easy decision.

Another way to manage the rockfall hazard is to climb through the risky pitches during or toward the end of a period of constant cold temperature. This, generally, means starting the scramble very early in the morning: welcome to the fraternity of the "alpine start!" An alpine start gets you out of your cozy sleeping bag at a time when most campers are polishing off their last beers by the campfire. Heading up the mountain at 4 am with

Assessing rockfall hazard

- Generally, if the mountain looks like a heap of rubble, watch for rockfall
- Once you are off the approach trail and on the route, stop and look around. Look on the ground for any rocks that look out of place—rocks may have landed on hard snow or ice, or seem to have fresh sharp edges. Rock that has been on the valley bottom for many years should be covered in lichens, soil or grass. Freshly detached rock from above should be bare.
- Look up to the surrounding walls and slopes: how fractured, crumbled or unstable do they appear? Look down gullies for alluvial and avalanche cones: when rock is washed free by water, snow or ice, it can pile up in these conical formations at the bottom of slopes.
- Grab the rock. Does it come apart easily and can you break it away from the face?
- Do you hear any rocks rolling down the slopes? Keep your ears open throughout the climb.
- Be aware that the rockfall hazard may change throughout the day as snow or ice melts and frees loose rock

only your headlamp and stubborn determination to guide you can put you on top of that rubble heap while the rocks are still bonded together with ice, or after the ice expansion has pried all the garbage loose. Once the rock has had some time in the midday sun, the ice bond will melt and free any unstable chunks. Just because you managed to climb up the most dangerous section at dawn doesn't mean you're safe for a midday descent. Western, then southern aspects experience the greatest diurnal temperature swings. At worst, the shaded southwestern facing couloir you climbed at 6 am, will be a gushing waterfall by 2 pm. If you have to downclimb or rappel it, you are vulnerable to rockfall and slippery, wet rock. If this looks like the scenario to come, the route is either out of condition, or you may be off-route. However, you may have studied the route for a day prior to your ascent and decided to climb a northeast gully that is shaded and frozen throughout the day. If you've taken the time to study the path of the sun and noticed the coming and going of shadows, you'll be able to anticipate the freeze/thaw cycle and choose the best line.

In some ranges, rockfall is an objective hazard 365 days of the year. In others, it may be worse during the seasonal transition from winter to spring. Aside from naturally occurring rockfall, scramblers (you included) can cause rockfall. On some of the busiest routes, people are the principle cause. Scrambling routes can be so steep that a rock knocked loose by a

Too many climbers on the route creates a prime environment for rockfall.

carelessly placed boot can fall or roll toward climbers below and gather enough velocity to cause serious, permanent or deadly injury. On some routes, it's virtually impossible to avoid causing minor rockfall. Therefore, care needs to be exercised to ensure that feet are placed for solid purchase. Additionally, climbers should avoid climbing directly above other members of their party. Of course, party members directly beneath the fall-line must be responsible for their own safety and ensure that they either stay out of the fall-line (sometimes impossible) or remain alert for rockfall.

I scrambled up Mt. Temple, near Lake Louise in the Canadian Rockies in 2004. It was a busy, fun and largely uneventful day until somebody screamed, "Rock!" As I was flattening myself against the slope, I caught sight of the careening boulder out of the corner of my eye. It was the size of a small microwave oven and heading straight toward me. Seconds later, someone gave the all-clear and we re-established upward progress as if nothing had happened. The rock had inadvertently been sent down by a party above us. There were so many people on the mountain, that this pandemonium continued for the rest of the day.

Frequently, if the rockfall hazard is high, scramblers will move one at a time through the fall-line. The higher climber may also yell to the lower whenever they move through the fall-line. A party of two or three may be able to climb close enough together that any one member is never below another. This way, two climbers are never in the fall-line at the same time.

If you're in the fall-line, the rocks will find you. *A hiker was enjoying his lunch directly beneath a rock face in the Lake Louise area of Alberta in 1976. A boulder fell and crushed his femur.*

Another frequent cause of rockfall is the improper management of climbing rope. You need to know how to anchor and retrieve rope to ensure that no rocks are dislodged, and how to rack and pass gear to other teammates.

Climbers try to use a common vocabulary when it comes to safety. If you hear someone yell, "Rock!," don't look up. Instead move your head and body into the slope. While climbing, become aware of potential hiding spots that can provide shelter from rockfall. Move quickly under an overhang or into a hollow. If no shelter is available, try to flatten yourself against the slope making as small a target as possible. Remember to keep your helmet level; don't bring your chin to your chest, as you will expose your neck. If you're able to pull your pack up to protect your neck, do it. Once someone yells, "Clear," or "Okay" it's safe to resume climbing. Remember, the cry of "Rock!" could also come from climbers below you who have seen or heard rockfall originating above you. Follow the same procedure every time. Practice to make your response automatic.

If you have knocked some rock loose and it's careening down, or if you see or hear rockfall, shout "Rock!" as loud as you can. If the rockfall has originated below you, or if climbers below have not reacted to your warning, keep yelling "Rock!" until they react, are out of danger or knocked unconscious. If you are stable and secure on the pitch, watch the path of the rock. Once the danger has past, give a shout of "Clear," or "Okay." Falling rock, ice or other objects (mostly bodies or gear) are the third leading cause of mountaineering accidents. It demands that climbers take every precaution to avoid it and quickly respond when it happens. Once again, wear a helmet!

Rockfall

- Rockfall is one of the leading causes of climbing accidents
- Wear a climbing helmet whenever the terrain is unstable, when climbing through gullies or couloirs, wherever there are signs of previous rockfall, on routes locally known for rockfall, when route descriptions in guidebooks warn of rockfall and whenever on a rope or belaying
- Understand enough of the geology of the area to determine the potential for unstable structures
- Warn other climbers on the route of any rockfall by yelling, "Rock!";
- Practice responding to "Rock!";
- When climbing, take extreme care to avoid causing rockfall. Don't walk up the route, but climb with consideration to other scramblers.
- If you're getting bombarded with rock from a party descending above you, pull over and let them pass. Better to have that group below you than above.
- Stay well-fed, hydrated and fit so you will be able to climb fast, thereby minimizing the time exposed to potential rockfall
- Manage ropes and gear to ensure you won't dislodge any rock
- Small parties may be able to climb together so that any scrambler-initiated rockfall will fall away from the party
- Larger parties should break into smaller groups if they can't climb as stated above

Avalanche

In the spring of 2000, two scramblers were attempting a peak near Field, British Columbia. They were climbing a south facing slope when a wet-snow avalanche carried one the party over a cliff. When he was rescued, he was found to have severe hypothermia and a critical leg injury. The spring conditions, daytime heating and the slope aspect all contributed to the incident.

The science of avalanche forecasting, and the skills and knowledge necessary to become competent in this complex discipline, are significantly beyond the scope of this book. Readers are urged to consult the reference list for additional texts. The discussion that follows is a mere brush stroke on a busy canvas, but it will serve the scrambler well.

Scramblers need to concern themselves with the snow that may remain when most scrambling routes are in condition, normally in the summer. During this time, avalanche forecasting centres are normally shut down. However, if you understand the nature of summer snow, and two simple principles, you'll be able to travel the backcountry with confidence:

- You must have an opinion regarding the stability of the snowpack. You can derive that opinion through your own assessment, or accept the opinion of a reliable source. Your opinion must be one of the following: there is no avalanche risk, there is an avalanche risk or the avalanche risk is unknown.

- You must be able to recognize avalanche-prone terrain.

If there is a risk of avalanche, or if the avalanche risk is unknown, you must avoid terrain that is in the start zone, path or run-out of any potential avalanche. Stated another way; if you are in a safe area, and will remain in safe terrain throughout your journey, then the avalanche risk doesn't matter.

Of course, nothing is ever that simple. If there is no avalanche risk, you still need to be cautious when travelling over summer snow. Summer snow changes much faster and more predictably than winter snow. The daily melt/freeze process will cause crystals to grow and compact, which contributes to

Avalanche safety tips

- Take an avalanche awareness course. Proper training and practice is required to be able to assess the stability of the snowpack
- Scramble when routes are in condition, not when they are still shaking off the winter's snow
- Heed avalanche warnings

Just before the winter's snow has stabilized, avalanches like this are common prior to routes coming into condition. Site of the avalanche in the gully of Mount Kidd. Photo: Sonny Bou.

stability. You can take advantage of this stability after a period of freezing, such as early in the morning. Beware of midday melting which can trigger wet-snow avalanches. Also, any fresh summer snow will require a couple days of melt/freeze to compact and stabilize.

If you stick to scrambling routes that are in condition, there should be no avalanche risk. As you gain experience, you'll benefit from an avalanche safety course. There are avalanche deaths every year in Canada. If mountains and mountaineering become your passion, you will, unfortunately, likely lose friends to avalanches. This need not be your destiny.

Three scramblers were descending from a successful summit of Mt. Kidd in Alberta's Kananaskis Country in the spring of 2004. Two members of the party glissaded past the third and soon triggered an avalanche. The wet-snow avalanche swept the two scramblers down the 40 metre-wide gully for approximately 500 metres. Everyone survived, however, one scrambler suffered a minor head injury and broken bones. Prior to their climb, the scramblers assessed the snowpack to be typical homogeneous summer snow, however, conditions proved to be more spring-like; wet-snow avalanches are common during these conditions.

Cornices

Cornices are a danger to mountain travellers whether they walk on or below them. These beautiful snow formations are created when wind-deposited snow accumulates on the lee side of ridges and peaks. The shape of the ridge or peak and its orientation to the prevailing wind will determine the size and extent of the cornices. If the terrain changes from lower angled to a sharp drop and runs perpendicular to the prevailing winds, cornicing will be relatively extensive.

The danger posed by cornices is that they eventually fracture and fall. Obviously, you don't want to be on the cornice when it lets go, nor would it be prudent to be travelling beneath it at that time. Looking up to ensure you are not in the fall-line of any large cornices is fairly easy. Determining the location of the fracture line in order to safely negotiate a corniced ridge is more problematic. A fracture may already exist, but the break in the snow at the location of the fracture may be covered by snow and unseen. The challenge for the climber and scrambler is to ensure that they travel below, that is, down from any potential fracture lines.

If you are able to see a fracture line, ensure you travel well below it, as there may be other ones that remain hidden. Normally, looking at the portion of the ridge that you've already travelled will give you a good impression of where the upcoming portions of the ridge might end, and the cornice begins. If you must approach the edge of the corniced feature, make sure you are belayed from a rock-solid anchor. This anchor must be bomber as it may need to bear the force of your fall plus the force of the cornice's collapse. These skills, and risks, are truly the realm of the experienced mountaineer and not of the scrambler. Beware.

New scramblers and climbers often underestimate this hazard. Cornices can stretch an incredible distance from terra firma. Photo: Dinah Kruze.

You can't always see all the snow from the trailhead. Both of these photographs of Mt. Cory were taken on the same day. The upper photograph was taken from the trailhead and the lower was taken just below the summit. Photo: Dave Stephens

Snow and ice

The second leading cause of mountaineering accidents is a slip or fall on snow or ice. You don't need to be in the Himalayas or three pitches up a six-pitch waterfall ice route in the Canadian Rockies to have to contend with slippery snow and ice. Most of the year, but certainly in spring and autumn, there is plenty of snow and ice around that can spell disaster for the unprepared scrambler. As with exposure, it's the consequences of a fall that determine how any snow-covered or icy terrain will be travelled. When confronted by this terrain, ask yourself these three questions:

1. Will a fall start you on an accelerated slide down the mountain?
2. If so, what will you hit along the way?
3. And, most importantly, where does the slope end (what obstacles are in the "run-out")?

For the first question, consider the steepness of the slope, whether the slope is covered with deep, soft snow or hard ice, and how little friction your clothing will exert. To answer question two, study the fall-line. Can you see every bit of terrain along the way and are you sure that there aren't any rock walls to hit, boulders or hidden cliff bands? Finally, where does the run-out end? Is there scree or talus waiting to chew up a misstepped scrambler, or crevasses in the fall-line?

Snow like this, frequently encountered near the summit, need not deter a trained scrambler. An ability to determine the stability of the snow and the competent use of an ice axe will help you manage this hazard. Photo: Andrew Nugara

Training and gear aside, what should you do if you encounter snow or ice? As a mountain hiker you've likely safely crossed snow before and hopefully the objective hazard, in your own judgment, was such that you felt the risk was negligible—right? If you were able to go back in time and run through the three questions listed above, would you make the same decision? If your answer is "Yes," great, you obviously exercised sound judgment. However, if you answered "No," that's good, too. Your answer tells me that you have learned something new and this book has provided some value.

Snow, under certain conditions, can accelerate your trek up the mountain. Normally, a half-day of training with a certified guide can teach you how to kick steps, plunge-step, self-arrest, self-belay, and best of all, glissade. Ice, however, should warn you of danger unless you've been trained and have practiced the required mountaineering skills to cross it safely. Beware of ice that has formed beneath the snow. Climbing snow-covered ice will normally have more in common with an alpine ice climb then a hike through a snowfield. Scrambling guidebooks in both North America and Europe often recommend the use of an ice axe for safe travel on certain routes. They may also suggest ropes, protection and crampons. Get some training and ensure you and your instructor are confident that you can competently use the equipment.

You need to know how to arrest a fall and do it as soon as possible. *A group of experienced climbers (no helmets or ice axes!) was descending a steep snow-filled gully in 1994. One member of the party slipped and slid down the gully striking rocks on the way down. She sustained a broken collarbone, dislocated shoulder, scalp lacerations and various cuts and bruises.*

If you encounter snow and ice

- All the key messages regarding avalanche hazard apply here
- Mountaineering training will enable you to safely travel over, up and down snow and ice
- Don't travel across any snow- or ice-covered terrain without asking yourself the three questions listed on page 40. It only takes a few seconds, and can truly save your life.

Snow-choked streambeds in gullies

As with all previous discussions regarding snow and ice, the slip, fall and sloughing hazard must be considered when venturing up or down snow-choked gullies.

The edges of a gulley offer some protection from rockfall, because you're out of the fall-line, and also have the option of handholds in rock. The edges, however, may not be the best choice if a layer of ice is found beneath the snow. This ice is normally created by the rapid melt/freeze cycle of the snow adjacent to the rock: the rock goes through a greater diurnal temperature swing than the snow in the centre of the gulley creating ice at the edges. But the centre may have the most stable, and, therefore, climbable, snow. It comes down to a situation-by-situation analysis. Always err on the side of caution.

Streams may be covered with snow for the entire summer. The probability of falling through the surface into a rushing torrent may evolve from minimal in the spring, to quite likely later in the season. Another hazard to beware of is the erosion of snow or ice stream banks. A common scenario is walking to the edge of the snow to get a better look at the stream, only to have the edge collapse. Having your pride soaked in freezing glacial meltwater may not be so bad when you consider that accidents such as these have ended in fatalities.

Two scramblers were descending unroped from a popular route near Lake Louise, Alberta in the spring of 1992. One fell through a small snow bridge to a hidden creek below. She died, likely of hypothermia or drowning.

Running ground water will melt or erode the snowpack from the bottom up. If you're crossing a snowfield and can hear the water rushing beneath you, take extra precautions: double-check the snow's ability to support you and your party, or consider belaying across the field.

Snow choked gullies, especially those with streams beneath them or deep holes can be very dangerous. Photo: Bob Spirko.

Objective hazards common to scrambling and hiking

Although these objective hazards receive minimum treatment in this book, it by no means minimizes the potential threat they can pose to mountain travellers. My assumption is, however, that readers are experienced hikers and are already able to manage these common backcountry hazards. If you'd like to learn more, please refer to the reference list at the back of the book, or take a backcountry skills course.

Fast or high water
It's often necessary for hikers to ford running water to reach their objective. For scrambling routes, fast water crossings will occur on approach. Hopefully your guidebook has mentioned a nearby bridge, the best place to cross or the time of year with the lowest water. If the water appears excessively high or fast, try looking upstream for minor tributaries. It's safer to cross several small watercourses than one raging river. Remember that most fit hikers can usually manage knee-deep, fast water. Deeper than this and many lighter or less experienced people may be knocked down; collapsible ski poles are handy here. Greater stability can also be gained by crossing in your boots, rather than in bare feet or sandals. Always ensure that you will be able to quickly remove your pack if the stream sweeps you off your feet by unbuckling your waist- and chest-belt before you venture across. If you need to cross water that is more than knee-deep, learn the crossing methods that are detailed in the books on the reference list. If you need to employ one of the more complex methods, it will help to practice the procedure before your life depends on it.

Access and remoteness
Why can access to the backcountry and the remoteness of the location be considered objective hazards? Referring back to the definition of objective hazard: objective hazards are those hazards that are present regardless of our presence in the mountains. Some scrambles require you only to park the car, walk a few steps to the base of the route and start climbing. Other approaches may involve hours or days spent on rough, poorly marked trails. The condition of those trails is what they are whether or not we're around to enjoy them. And the additional equipment and planning that a long and difficult approach may require will need to be addressed well in advance.

The same can be said for the remoteness of a location. Think of the ease of egress. If an accident occurs in a remote location and you require additional help beyond what you and your partners can manage, you may be out of luck. By the time someone hikes back to the trail, it may be too late. Much of the backcountry in North America sees little if any human

travel. It's important that you are comfortable with the feeling of isolation that comes with wilderness mountaineering. Furthermore, it's absolutely critical that you are a fully self-sufficient party. Some remote parks in the Arctic require backcountry travellers to demonstrate self-reliance by having an emergency response plan that will dispatch rescue, normally at your expense! The ability to call for help brings us to one final consideration: the availability of wireless communications infrastructure.

Availability of wireless communications

The responsible use of radios, cellular and satellite phones should be made crystal clear: just because you can call for help doesn't mean you can forgo self-sufficiency. If you, or anyone else, has a serious or life-threatening injury that prohibits them from safely getting out of the backcountry, even if helped by other members of the group, then call for help. The ability to spark up the cellular phone may be the difference between life and death. Relying on that same phone as the only element of your emergency response plan, however, could have dire consequences.

Of course, getting a cellular signal is not always possible in the backcountry of North America. I've also brought radios into the mountains and have experienced disappointment with their reception and transmission, mostly due to signal problems caused by terrain. I now carry a satellite phone. So far, the most important call I've had to make was to a restaurant in Banff; we were running a couple hours late and I needed to change the dinner reservations. I have tested the satellite phone many times in the backcountry and have always had a good enough signal to make a call, but I still never rely on it. The cost of this technology has recently come down to the point where frequent backcountry travellers can justify the expenditure. If you can't justify the purchase, you may be able to rent one. Call your local climbing club or a guide association for rental referrals.

Mountain weather

Those of us who live in and near the mountains understand the nature of the weather—constant change. As the saying goes, "If you don't like the weather, wait five minutes!" Scrambling routes, when compared to hiking trails, are characterized by increased exposure and commitment. In this regard, the scrambler must be more vigilant and respond appropriately to changes in weather. Furthermore, scramblers must mimic the behaviour of alpine climbers by seriously considering whether or not to abort or retreat from a climb if conditions become unfavourable.

You never know where you'll be when the weather hits. Be ready.

A group of scramblers was traversing a popular peak near Canmore, Alberta in 2001. While they were taking a break on the summit, a storm blew in. They became disoriented and started to descend via the incorrect route. The group became stranded above dangerous cliff bands. Rescuers were able to climb to the group by midnight, provide warm sleeping bags and start a fire. The members of this hypothermic group were helicoptered out in the morning.

Mountain weather is characterized by extremes of temperature, wind and precipitation. One statement holds true for every season in any mountain

Competent scramblers prepared for the weather. Photo: Dave Stephens.

Mountain weather

- Learn about mountain weather in general and the patterns specific to your local climbing area
- Find a reliable weather forecasting service and learn to interpret the reports
- Learn first aid for cold and heat injuries
- Learn the mechanisms of heat transfer and how to protect yourself against heat loss
- Invest in the minimum of lightweight mountain clothing that will protect you from severe weather
- Protect yourself from the increased UVB radiation present at higher elevations
- Don't scramble in the rain
- Understand the damage caused by severe thunderstorm winds and how to protect yourself from harm
- Learn how to reduce the probability of being struck by lightning
- Abort the climb if the weather conditions become extreme or if you are not prepared for potentially dangerous conditions

range: the higher you climb, the colder it gets—active volcanoes spouting lava are the exception. Starting a climb on a chilly late-summer morning and finding the temperature on the summit to be quite balmy by early afternoon is not contrary to the previous statement, as the temperature in the valley is likely proportionally warmer, too. There is normally a 4 °C to 6 °C temperature decrease for every 1000 m (3,300 ft) increase in elevation. Combine the drop in temperature with high winds, as wind speed also increases with an increase in elevation, and you may have a serious objective hazard to manage.

When we travel in a horizontal world, we modify our behaviour to account for potential changes in weather and/or climate. If travelling from London to Palm Beach for some winter renewal, we expect a warmer climate and pack our suitcase accordingly. This same planning needs to be done for the vertical weather changes of mountaineering—regardless if a trip takes a few hours or a few days. Scramblers need to be able to recognize the signs of changing weather conditions and then take the necessary precautions. Packing the right clothing to combat foul weather can be a lifesaver.

However, the weight of packing all the hats, mittens and sweaters for the absolute coldest possible temperature will slow your vertical progress and prolong your exposure to all objective hazards. You need to find the right balance between weight and environmental protection. Later, I'll discuss packing for an uncomfortable survival.

Heat transfer

At this stage of our weather discussion, some thermodynamic theory is needed: As I sit comfortably in front of my computer, I'm in thermodynamic balance with respect to my environment and my level of exertion. If the temperature in the room increases, or if I start to exercise, I will no longer be in balance and I would start to feel warmer.

Similarly, if I opened the window and allowed a blast of icy winter air to fill the room, heat would be transferred from my body to this new, colder environment. If these "unbalanced" conditions are not managed, I would become uncomfortable and, in extreme scenarios, I would die! Heat transfer, and therefore cooling, occurs by way of one or any combination of the following heat-transfer processes: conduction, convection, evaporation and radiation.

Conduction

Heat transfer by the process of conduction occurs when direct contact is created between objects of dissimilar temperature. Scramblers are affected by conductive heat loss whenever they touch something cold. The most common sources are the soles of climbing boots touching cold rock, the soles of boots connected to cold crampons, hands holding a cold ice axe, sitting on cold ground and grasping a metal fuel bottle at -40 °C/F with bare hands. Wet clothing pressed against the body will also contribute to conductive cooling. Poorly vasculated regions of the body are particularly vulnerable to rapid cooling: I've had a friend get a frostbitten knee from a few minutes of kneeling to rummage through his pack. Be vigilant!

Convection

Heat transfer by convection occurs by the movement of a fluid: movement of air in the mountains and water in the case of being immersed. (Evaporative heat loss, discussed later, is somewhat different than convective heat loss.) The greatest factor contributing to convective heat loss in the mountains is wind, and it's one of the leading causes of hypothermia. The body will try to warm the layer of air that is next to the skin. Therefore, even the smallest air exchange within non-windproof clothing can have a significant cumulative effect as the body repeatedly tries to re-warm that layer of air.

Evaporation

Evaporation is caused by a loss of energy (heat) as a fluid (perspiration) changes from a liquid to a vapour. If you need to prove this physical law and solicit a few strange looks just lick the back of your hand and then blow on it. Feels cool, doesn't it? The air from your lungs is near 100 per cent relative humidity. The wet spot would feel even colder if you blew dry air on it. The air is dryer at high elevations than at sea level. Therefore, a

The comings and goings of weather on Mt. Crandell. Photo: Dave Stephens.

cool breeze lofting across your sweat-soaked back when you remove your pack can contribute to major heat loss if left unchecked. This process is known as evaporative cooling and is also a significant source of heat loss during the transfer of moisture to cold air breathed into your lungs. Breathing cold, dry air in the lungs will lower the body's core temperature. Preheating the air by using a balaclava or face mask can help, but good hydration is the best defence.

Radiation
Heat transfer by the process of radiation occurs when heat is radiated to some colder object or environment. The greater the temperature differences between the heat source and the colder object, the greater the rate of heat transfer. Radiant heat transfer is a continuous process to which we seem to be physiologically unaware during the course of our daily lives. In the mountains, however, it can be a killer. For some more strange looks, hold a bag of frozen vegetables a few centimetres from your face and feel the heat transfer. That cold feeling is created by the increased radiant heat loss from your face to this new, colder object in your environment. Now imagine the potential heat transfer between your body and a cold, granite mountain.

Temperature extremes

- Take time to learn and understand weather forecasts
- Invest in effective lightweight mountain clothing
- Confront your reluctance to call off the scramble due to weather conditions. Like most things in life, your behaviour is influenced by fear. Act smart, not scared.
- Learn to recognize and treat cold and heat illness
- Recognize and respond to excessive wind (convective cooling)
- Recognize and respond to objects in your environment that draw excessive heat from your body (radiant cooling)
- Insulate yourself from cold surfaces as necessary (conductive cooling)
- Impede evaporative cooling to stay warm
- Promote evaporative cooling to stay cool
- Use your head, literally. Wearing or removing a hat will have a significant effect on your comfort.
- Keep yourself hydrated, well-fed and fit

One of the greatest hazards encountered in a crevasse-fall is the subsequent effect of massive radiant heat loss to the surrounding walls of ice. To the scrambler, managing radiant heat loss is more than an awareness of the necessity to keep warm, it also includes carefully choosing a belay location, a bivouac site and even a proper location to have lunch. If you know you'll be stationary for some time, like when you are belaying or stopping for a snack, be conscious of the potential for significant radiant heat loss to caves, waterfalls and large boulders.

Overheating

Until now, we have only discussed heat transfer from the perspective of becoming too cold, but what about becoming too hot? Although I haven't fallen while scrambling or suffered a cold injury, I have been seriously afflicted with heat illness, twice! Both times were in the Rocky Mountains of Western Canada and, both times were entirely preventable.

The treatment afforded the subject of over-heating need not be as detailed as the previous discussion of cooling: an understanding of heat transfer will serve us well in the discussion of hyperthermia (the condition of having a body temperature dangerously above normal). The principal mechanism of cooling (heat transfer) employed by the human body is evaporation.

Evaporative cooling is the result of the energy of vaporization; that is, the giving off of heat as liquid sweat changes to a gas. This brings us to the understanding that the production of sweat is critical to this cooling process. And, since the production of sweat is critical, and therefore, encouraged, the scrambler must ensure he remains well-hydrated.

My first encounter with a heat-related injury was directly attributable to inadequate hydration. Scrambling on a hot August day, we were pushed for time so we carried a minimum amount of water to keep our packs as light as possible. That was stupid. We managed to summit, but I barely managed to stumble back to my truck. It took thirty minutes for my resting heart rate to drop below 125 beats per minute and another two hours for it to drop below 100 beats per minute. The temperature that day remained above 30 °C for the duration of the hike, and I had only consumed one half-litre of water.

The second incident was attributable to both inadequate hydration and the impeding of evaporative cooling. Remember, severe heat injury can result in death. Forcing yourself to consume enough water that will result in consistently straw-coloured urine can truly mean the difference between life and death. Additionally, regulating clothing and physical activity in response to being excessively hot will create a more pleasurable and safer mountain experience. Not only is an "alpine start" some insurance against rockfall and avalanches, it can put you on and off the peak before the heat of the day hits.

Hydration
Many ailments experienced by active hikers, scramblers and climbers can be minimized, if not prevented, with proper hydration. On a strenuous scramble, you can lose over one litre of liquid per hour! Therefore, replacing all of the water as it is being lost to the environment is virtually impossible. The best that scramblers can do is ensure adequate hydration prior to the climb, do their best to drink as much as possible during the climb and concentrate on hydration for a few days after.

A few tips on keeping topped-up

- Recognize the signs and symptoms of dehydration: muscle cramps, headaches, abnormal fatigue
- Don't hydrate with sugar or the popular sport drinks. Stick to water or the water-supplements used by the pros (likely not the drinks you're thinking of).
- Don't rely on your thirst to prompt you to drink. Force yourself to drink at predetermined intervals: every 50 m of elevation, every fifteen minutes, etc.
- Start drinking lots of water a day or two prior to your climb

Precipitation

Precipitation increases with an increase in elevation. In coastal ranges, the increase in precipitation is linear with respect to elevation gain: there will be twice the precipitation at 3000 m as there is at 1500 m. The increase in precipitation in interior ranges, however, tends to be exponential: there will be more than twice the precipitation at 3000 m as there is at 1500 m. Of course, precipitation may come in the form of rain, snow or hail; all of which are an objective hazard for mountain travellers. Spring and summer rain might also include the most dangerous byproduct of precipitation: rockfall! If it's raining, or about to, don't go scrambling. Not only do you have to be wary of rockfall caused by the rain's erosive power weakening any dirt or ice bonds, but any hand- or footholds will be too slippery. A good downpour may also wash out any signs of a trail, and if the rain is heavy enough, streams may become impassable or suddenly appear in a once-dry gully.

Hail will produce similar problems as rain. Snow may result in avalanche hazard. Even if the accumulation is not sufficient to cause avalanches, your footing on slippery rock will be even more precarious than if it had only rained, especially if the rock is covered with moss or lichen.

Cold temperatures and precipitation can also produce the conditions required for verglas to form. Verglas is a thin film of ice that covers rock and creates a hazard similar to black ice on a highway. It's virtually impossible to climb verglas without crampons, and crampons will only provide marginal assistance.

We backpacked the Chilkoot Trail in 2002. On the second night it started to rain—Alaska-size rain. Undeterred, on the morning of day three we began the scramble over Chilkoot Pass. As we passed treeline, we noticed that the small streams we had intended to hop across had become raging torrents. We retreated to high ground above our washed-out camp. What a smart decision. On the morning of day four, with barely a drop of rain for twelve hours, the two-metre-deep torrents had become boot-deep trickles again. What a difference a day makes!

Precipitation

- Don't embark on a climb while it's raining
- If there is a possibility of rain, carry an ultra-lightweight waterproof jacket for the retreat or to wear while waiting out the storm
- Be prepared (by donning your helmet) for rockfall caused by rain or heavy, wet snow
- Understand the conditions required for the formation of verglas and avoid them

Severe wind

The greatest hazard posed by high winds is severe cooling. Refer to the earlier section on heat transfer mechanisms for more detail. This discussion will focus on other hazards posed by strong winds.

As mentioned earlier, wind velocity increases with corresponding increases in elevation. Mountain terrain can direct wind around features and through narrow passages. A col between two snowcapped peaks may look like a divine spot to pitch a tent, but it's likely the windiest spot. The adjacent peaks will direct the coming breeze right through the narrow passage. Severe winds, like those accompanied by thunderstorms, can dislodge rocks and fall trees, not to mention blow you right off the mountain—it has happened. *Alison Hargreaves, a 33-year-old high-altitude mountaineer, was blown off the summit ridge of K2 by gale-force winds in 1995. Her body rests somewhere on the mountain.*

Even a seemingly minor wind-perpetuated annoyance, such as flying particulate gritting up the eyes, may impair a scrambler's vision enough to force retreat or rescue. Another danger caused by strong wind is a blow-down: a section of terrain subject to a significant wind event that causes trees to be blown to the ground. Though this is not a hazard encountered on scrambling routes, it can be present as an obstacle on approach, especially in areas that have been burned.

Always be prepared for changing conditions. Mountain winds can result in cold injuries in the middle of the summer or create whiteout conditions under a clear blue sky. Photo: Andrew Nugara.

Most dangerous wind conditions originate from thunderstorms. It is critical that climbers learn to evaluate weather forecasts. Once in the mountains, it actually becomes easier to assess changing cloud patterns, but by then you may need to make a quick decision. At the trailhead, most people will try to convince themselves that the weather "doesn't look too bad," or say, "If it gets any worse, we'll just turn around." The reluctance to call off a climb after you've packed the night before, gotten out of bed at 4 am and driven an hour to the trailhead, must be managed. If you spend enough time in the mountains, you're going to be faced with potentially life-threatening weather that you must address with positive actions.

Severe wind

When coping with poor mountain weather, knowledge, preparation and good judgment are required. When faced with severe mountain winds, heed these precautions:

- Understand how topography influences the direction and velocity of wind. Winds will be funnelled through narrow passages.
- Understand the potential force of mountain winds—especially those accompanying thunderstorms. Beware of rockfall.
- Carry a light windproof jacket to limit evaporative cooling
- Carry sunglasses or goggles to protect your eyes from suspended dust and dirt
- You may not be safe in a tent; severe mountain winds have lifted tents off the ground
- If the topography does not provide any obvious shelter, stay low and protect your head and face

Thunder and lightning

My wife and I were descending Cascade Mountain in Canada's Banff National Park at around 1 pm on July 22, 2003. We had spent about 90 minutes on the summit—we believe in a summit nap—after which I noticed some larger cloud formations building in the west and moving towards us. As we'd had a good amount of time on the summit, I thought it wise to begin the descent. As we approached treeline, I heard a high-pitched buzzing. I stopped and asked my wife if she also heard the sound. She turned her head and leaned towards me, "It's your ice axe," she said. In an instant, we threw our axes and ski poles 20 ft to our side, crouched down and covered our ears with our hands. Within seconds, thunder roared and it began to hail. We sat that way for about ten minutes as the storm passed. We didn't see any lightning, but to say we were nervous would be an understatement.

The scenario on Cascade Mountain is a poor example of thunderstorm forecasting; I wouldn't suggest it. The weather was supposed to be clear and sunny that day. I didn't hear any warnings of thunderstorm activity on the radio weather reports. But I also didn't check my favourite Internet weather resources prior to driving to the park.

In memory of a scrambler struck by lightning. Photo: Gillean Daffern.

Lightning kills livestock and people—climbers included—every year. *A man was found dead on the top of Mount Fairview, near lake Louise, Alberta in 2002. Public safety officers figured that he was just sitting there during a lightning storm and was struck. It is suspected that the storm moved in suddenly during a period of clear weather.*

The single most dangerous and life-threatening element of a thunderstorm is lightning. In Western Canada, thunderstorms are common in late spring and early summer. Farther east into the prairies, they can be a threat until late summer. If you understand how and when thunderstorms form in your locale, you can plan climbs around the storms, thereby limiting your chances of exposure to the hazard.

See the reference list for an excellent book about lightning and thunderstorms.

Dealing with thunderstorms

- Learn about mountain weather and thunderstorms
- Remember that lightning can strike from clouds that are 5 – 8 km away (3 – 5 miles). You need to be farther than this from the storm to be safe
- Lightning can strike the same place twice (or more)
- To reduce the chance of being struck by lightning, don't be the tallest object around and don't be near the tallest object.
- If you're in water, get out. If you're near water, get away.
- Don't keep metal objects nearby. Toss your pack, axe, crampons, ski poles and hardware at least 15 ft away. If you hear a buzzing sound or see arcing or flashing (St. Elmo's Fire) take immediate action.
- Seek shelter in lower areas such as valleys or lower down on the slope. Beware of holes and shallow caves, ground currents can find you there.
- If you're caught in the open, crouch down with your feet together and cover your ears to protect your hearing from thunder. Don't lie down or spread your feet apart. The jury is still out on whether or not sitting on an insulating object, like a pack or foam mat, offers protection. The voltage of a lightning strike could blast right through them. If it feels good, do it—but make sure there's no metal in the pack.

Understanding subjective hazards

Unlike objective hazards, subjective hazards can be controlled, managed, reduced and changed. Regardless of the severity of any objective hazard, it's really the subjective hazards that control our safety in the mountains. In other words, we control our own safety in the mountains. While other mountaineering texts may list additional subjective hazards, I have chosen to discuss only four.

Skill
Knowledge and the ability to competently execute specific techniques are required to minimize the adverse consequences of objective hazards. This is called skill. Skills can be learned and practiced. A section in this book will discuss the skills necessary for safe scrambling. With respect to the concept of subjective hazards, however, a level of skill is translated to ability. Scrambling within your abilities is safer and more enjoyable than exceeding your abilities. It also allows us to enjoy scrambling while we increase our ability and accumulate experience. Be honest with yourself and others regarding your level of climbing ability.

Experience
Through the repeated application of skill (practice), the scrambler also gains experience. In his book, *Extreme Alpinism: Climbing Light, Fast and High*, Mark Twight discusses climbing as an experience-oriented sport rather than goal-oriented sport. Fixation on the summit can cloud your judgment and deprive you of an opportunity to learn and build experience. A climber who is focused on the experience will learn and grow in skill much faster than a climber whose only recollection of a route is the summit. Focusing on the summit, to a certain degree, is important to maintaining motivation, but not at the expense of awareness and safety.

Like it or not, experience is paid for with time. The quality of that time is largely within your control. If you spend enough time climbing mountains, you will become familiar with success as well as failure. Draw knowledge from each. Making the same mistake more than once, or repeatedly misinterpreting the same information, demonstrates a lack of awareness. Building experience is a never-ending process, so you might as well enjoy it. Experience can also be viewed in terms of an apprenticeship. Journeymen train apprentices. As you progress to more difficult routes, you will encounter obstacles that require yo to employ skill, knowledge or gear in excess of your current competency. At this fork in the road, you must decide if you will avoid such challenges or work to overcome them. If you choose to work on the problem, you are faced with yet another decision: do you attempt to climb the pitch or retreat and seek advice or training? Both may be valid choices. The former will contribute greatly to your well of experience; however, the risk may prove prohibitive. Here, I advocate training.

Two scramblers attempted a peak near the townsite of Banff, Alberta in 1996. The route was listed as 3rd class with a short, steep section that could be avoided. At the steep section, one climber turned back and the other continued. The lower climber heard a scream and found his partner dead at the base of the steep pitch.

Judgment

A previous discussion of judgment was included as part of the comparison between hiking and scrambling. Therefore, only a brief summary of the subject is included here.

New scramblers are often confronted with circumstances not previously experienced. In these situations, they must use their judgment to decide whether they should continue upward or retreat. Judgment is a decision based on an accurate assessment of your ability to safely overcome new challenges, given your level of skill and experience. Good judgment helps you avoid danger. Bad judgment can cost you your life. Each person's judgment should be respected, even if you strongly disagree with it. For example, your decision that the storm will pass may conflict with another's belief that the party should abort the climb due to the storm. However, even if you are the most "qualified" member of the party to make such determinations, everyone's opinion should be respected and considered, even if not accepted. The ability to honestly consider the opinions of others demonstrates the humility that every mountain traveller must possess in order to be a lifelong student of the mountains.

Ed Viesturs, a professional high-altitude mountaineer, stood on the upper slopes of Annapurna in Nepal in the spring of 2002. Viesturs and his climbing partner, despite the hopes of their sponsors and other supporters, made a decision to abort the climb in the face of what they considered to be an extreme objective hazard. Two other climbers, however, continued to the summit and were successful. In *Himalayan Quest*, Viesturs wrote: "During the preceding weeks, the winds had deposited a huge amount of snow, and on the day we arrived we found a textbook avalanche slope. For Veikka [Gustafsson] and myself, the level of risk was unacceptable. Jean-Christophe [Lafaille] and Alberto [Inurrategi] chose to continue and they successfully reached the summit a few days later. We were comfortable with our decision. It was a disappointment, to be sure, but we both plan to find another way up."

I can imagine that the pressure on Viesturs and Gustafsson to continue must have been incredible. This makes their decision not to continue even more courageous.

Not a place I'd like to be without a solid belay. Good judgment and a healthy fear of dying are great items to pack for a difficult scramble. Photo: Dave Stephens.

Self-knowledge

The ability to exercise good judgment requires self-knowledge. Only by understanding your ambition, motivation and biases, can you make a more objective appraisal of the situation and minimize the emotional influence inherent in the decision-making process. Attitudes toward risk and risk tolerance need to be understood and communicated to your climbing partner(s). Your reason for scrambling is likely difficult, if not impossible, to articulate. But your goals should be discernible. Make sure everyone in the climbing party is reading from the same book and on the same page as you. Before you leave the approach and head up the route, there should be agreement regarding the ultimate goal of the climb: is it the summit at all costs, to get some exercise or is it just to determine whether the route is within your ability? There is nothing worse than getting to the crux and learning that you're the only one who wants to continue.

Avoid becoming a victim of the subjective

When a scrambler needs to make a decision regarding an objective hazard, there are only three possible answers: continue to climb; stop, wait, reassess then maybe find a way to manage the hazard; retreat. A bad, if not wrong, decision will result in some failure. The magnitude of failure, however, can vary greatly from not enjoying the rest of the climb to someone being injured or killed. Wrong decisions that place scramblers in a situation where they do not have the required skill and experience to continue up or down are the product of poor judgment. Bad judgment, resulting in the wrong decision, is the leading cause of mountaineering accidents. Acquiring self-knowledge will help you understand why you made that decision. Furthermore, having the courage and determination to improve and change will break the chain of poor judgment and result in increasing success as a mountaineer.

Accident scenario

Two scramblers were descending by a direct route, avoiding the easier trail normally used by most who ascend the peak. Their new route took them over increasingly steeper terrain and slabs of rock covered with smaller, loose rocks. One of them slipped down a steep slab stopping just a few metres short of a terminal drop. Unable to assist his partner down the mountain, the other scrambler went for help. The next morning, the stranded scrambler was slung out by helicopter.

Injuries: hypothermia; badly bruised and skinned.

What can be learned from this?

- Most mountaineering accidents happen on descent. Scramblers should descend by familiar routes; the most obvious being their ascent route.
- Down-sloping terrain tends to obscure successively steeper terrain i.e.: you can't see if there is a cliff or how far the next drop will be.
- A slip on the rock caused the climber to fall farther down the slope. The proper use of a rope and belay could have arrested the fall.
- Small rocks that lay on smooth slabs will act as tiny ball bearings on those slabs and are frequently the cause of slips and falls.
- This accident happened in the summer. As the victim waited overnight for rescue, he was not able to prevent the onset of hypothermia. Scramblers should be equipped to survive a night in the mountains without incurring further injury.

Group dynamics

Have you ever had an argument with your spouse or close friend while on a hike? Hopefully it was short and didn't ruin the day. Tension between scramblers, whether the tension is known to the team or is unrecognized, can spoil an otherwise beautiful day in the mountains. At its extreme, it can cause or contribute to an accident or fatality.

The dynamics that create tension are complex. A psychological study of climbers' personalities would no doubt yield interesting, if not disturbing, results. If you are an avid hiker who is now drawn to scrambling, you're likely interested in even more adventurous mountaineering, such as ice or rock climbing. You might describe yourself as motivated. Perhaps your friends or family might describe you as driven. Would a not-so-kind acquaintance call you obsessive? I think I'll stop this line of inquiry. What I'm getting at is that we all bring our personality into the mountains. It's unavoidable … it's acceptable, too. It is unacceptable, however, to let your personality spoil the fun for others or endanger them. Whether you are scrambling with your spouse, date, son, daughter, parent or friend, you have a personal responsibility to contribute to the safety of the group, to contribute to the enjoyment of the outing and to help others do the same.

Leave any personal baggage at the trailhead. It's all about respect. Respect for others who are less skilled. Respect for the slower members of the group. Respect for the fact that someone is nervous or scared. Temper your schedule or objective accordingly. Always respect the request for a rope or belay. And most of all, respect yourself: you are allowed to be tired or nervous. You deserve respect when you tell someone that they need to slow down or that you would rather call it a day than cross that final exposed ridge. You deserve to have a good time, too.

The points detailed above become even more relevant as scrambling parties become larger than two or three members. Someone may need to be the big "L": Leader. The leader need not be the fittest or most skilled climber, but should be the best decision maker and communicator. Remember, however, that in the end, climbing and scrambling are characterized by personal responsibility. If you haven't hired a professional guide and charged them with the role of leader, then you are truly responsible for your own actions.

Keep your party together

Whether hiking or scrambling, keeping a party together should be one of the group's highest priorities. Separation can be necessary during an emergency, but it should not be the norm. Good groups will ensure that all members understand the advantages of keeping together, however, they will also ensure that each individual is prepared for any unplanned separation.

Mountaineering accidents are full of scenarios where separation has been one of the main causes. Typically, individuals will make different decisions alone than when they are part of a group. They may take more, or less, risk. Keeping your party together may not ensure that you make the best decisions, but hopefully, other members may challenge the obviously wrong ones. Don't forget about errors in route finding. One group may end up on the wrong route or trail necessitating a lengthy search or dangerous rescue.

In 1996, two scramblers found themselves directly below the vertical crux of a popular local peak near Banff, Alberta. One scrambler decided that the piece was too difficult and decided to turn back. The other scrambler continued upward, only to fall to his death from the 10 m vertical pitch. These two scramblers were, obviously, both confident in their decisions and determined enough to follow through. If they had tried harder to stay together, the outcome would likely have been different: they both could have returned to the parking lot, both could have summited, or worse, both could have died.

My partners and I have faced these types of decisions many times. It normally results in someone leading to belay the other, or we head back to the car for an early lunch.

Avoid becoming separated

- Make sure everyone knows the agreed-upon emergency procedure
- Make sure all members of the party know where they are and where they're trying to go
- Members of the group, other than the trip "leader," should have maps and be able to navigate to and from the objective
- If you do lose members along the way, stop. Abort your objective until you find them. Always search in pairs.
- If someone wants to abort the scramble and descend to the parking lot, make sure they don't go back alone

Clothing and a few extras

If you've been hiking or backpacking for any length of time, you are likely aware of the available variety of clothing fabrics and designs. Assuming that you already know how to select mountain clothing, this chapter discusses the specific requirements of scrambling clothing: lightweight, effective enough to keep you alive and provide comfort, but not luxury. Luxury is heavy. Also included here is a short discussion of a few essential gear items and a couple of extras worthy of consideration.

Feet first
The boots worn by most hikers and backpackers are a poor choice for scrambling. Even the heavier models will disadvantage the scrambler with their flexibility, lack of ankle support and poor abrasion protection. The best boots for scrambling are leather mountaineering boots designed for summer temperatures. Within the range of choices, a scrambler's requirements will normally be satisfied with the lighter, not heavier and bulkier, models. The midsole will be stiff enough to enable a secure purchase on small footholds with minimal calf muscle fatigue, and the leather uppers will be stiff and high enough to support your ankles over uneven terrain. The lighter models should also provide hours of pain-free approach hikes. These boots will likely be stiff enough to take an articulating (flexible) crampon. Boots intended for hiking are too flexible, causing the metal crampon frame to fatigue and break.

   I don't blister and bleed like I used to when I break-in boots —and I'm sure I'm not the only person with this new luxury. My feet haven't changed, but the quality of the mountain footwear has. When shopping for boots, fit, of course, is everything. It took me about six hours to buy my last pair of boots. I tried on so many models, and various sizes of each, that I got blisters—not on my feet, but on my hands and fingers as a result of having to lace up so many times that day! When I put on the last pair, I immediately knew they were the ones. Expect to find the perfect fitting boots and try everything until you do. If you are still dissatisfied after many hours or days of boot trials, then you'll need to settle for the most comfortable of the lot. Maybe you can get them modified. I've modified my own marginally comfortable boots, but I know a professional can do a better job. Before you wear the boots outdoors, take them to a good shoe repair shop that specializes in modifications for hard-to-fit feet. If the technician is confident that the boots can be modified for a comfortable fit, you'll have to decide if it's worth the risk. Remember, they can't be returned once cut, glued or otherwise tampered with.

Wind, rain and snow

No fabric provides the combination of water repellency and breathability that will keep you dry while working hard. If it is adequately breathable, the rain and snow will likely soak through. If it's genuinely waterproof, you'll sweat to the point of dehydration or hyperthermia. Scrambling in the rain is extremely dangerous, so you would not be planning a trip where you're needing protection from a thoroughly waterproof garment.

The question becomes: how dry do you really need to be and how much sweating can you safely handle? You will be well-served with two jackets: one that is waterproof and one that is windproof. Both should be breathable, but to different degrees, and both need to be as lightweight as possible. This combination will be more effective, lighter and cheaper than the latest super-fabric alternative.

All climbing is exhausting. If you're having an easy time, you're likely going too slow and should consider speeding up to reduce the time you are exposed to objective hazards of the mountain environment. You should be sweating. High winds can hasten evaporative cooling to the point where hypothermia can become a threat, even on a sunny summer day. If a mist or a light shower develops, you'll likely be warm enough wearing your wind jacket to evaporate the light precipitation. I have a micro-fibre jacket and pants. Each weighs about as much as a roll of film. They work wonderfully in light precipitation.

When the rain begins to pound, it's time to pull over or retreat. I carry an unlined, hardly breathable, nearly entirely waterproof and extremely lightweight jacket. Best of all, it was cheap. I normally don't bring water repellent pants on summer scrambles. If I'm able to climb, or I'm hiking out, my wind pants or climbing pants will suffice. If it's pouring and I'm hunkered down, I'll be wrapped up in my bivy bag. Leave those heavy, bulky and expensive super-fabric coats at home, saving them for cold snowy weather. If you do buy some new clothing, choose brighter colours rather than the popular greens and blues. In the unlikely event that you'll need rescue, orange or yellow is more easily seen from a helicopter.

Insulation

You'll need to know the lowest temperature that can be expected at night. I carry my insulation for that unplanned bivouac. If it's September in the Canadian Rockies, I can expect daytime temperatures of 30 °C (90 °F) and chilly nights as low as 0 °C (32 °F), or colder. That said, I'm not going to weigh myself down with enough insulation to make me comfortable. Plan to suffer, but not to freeze to death … you don't want the sound of your chattering teeth frightening the bears. For most of the scrambling season, a fleece jacket, or a lighter garment of comparable warmth, will do. (Hint: try to find something lighter than standard pile fleece.) I'll pack a light

One piece of light insulation, like this down jacket, can make a cold mountain feel like a tropical beach.

down jacket when the nightly temperature is guaranteed to go below 0 °C (32 °F). That may not sound too cold by mountain standards, but when you're tired, hungry and dehydrated, you're at risk.

Accessorize

The higher you climb, the more intense the UV radiation. Take all those sun protection items that smart hikers carry. Also, consider carrying a wool or fleece hat at any time of the year: it will keep you warm on a windy ridge when it's snowing in August! A pair of wool or fleece gloves is also a good idea for the bottom of your pack. I throw in waterproof mitt shells once the weather starts to cool.

I used to scramble in shorts, light nylon-ish pants or running tights for colder days. A few years ago, I discovered the merits of real climbing pants. I now have two pairs I use for scrambling. One is made of Schoeller Dryskin; I wear these when I might expect snow or a bit of rain. The other pair is made of the toughest fabric I've found to date. Most manufacturers of climbing clothing make pants like these—and fabric technology will, no doubt, continue to evolve.

Climbing helmet

Climbing helmets are designed to either deform or destruct upon impact. Each design has its advantages and disadvantages and the proponents of both designs occupy equal ground. I prefer the deforming design. It has a bigger profile and looks a little more clunky, but it's a design I feel can sustain rough treatment and multiple impacts—even if my head and neck might not. In the reference list you'll find two "must reads" that will help you choose a helmet. The section on objective hazards discusses rockfall and exposure: an appreciation of both should convince you of the helmet's necessity.

Use the gear you have to get your body off the cold ground. Then, loosen your boots or remove them if they're wet, and crawl inside the bivy bag wearing your warmest clothes.

ʋy bag
ɪs a bivy bag a luxury? If you've carried the appropriate clothing and informed a responsible person of your location and return time, then you really should be able to spend one sufficiently uncomfortable and introspective night before you're rescued or walk out. So why carry that extra weight? To start with, there are minimalist bivy bags that are very light. Secondly, the shelter and warmth that they afford is truly worth their diminutive weight and minor bulk. If you are injured, if the weather turns ugly, if you're lost, or have damaged or soaked your clothing, the bivy bag will bridge a gap and could save your life. A brightly coloured bag can be used to signal a helicopter; I've seen some orange bags, made of thin nylon, with "HELP" written across them. When shopping for a bivy sac, look at all the models and choose the lightest. If it occupies more space than a warm pair of mittens, it's too big.

Headlamps
A lightweight LED (light emitting diode) headlamp is a great addition to your pack. It will only take as much space as a roll of film and weighs about the same. Many of the newer models have the capability to function as strobes: a great locating beacon whether it's day or night. Remember to keep those batteries fresh!

Extras
Most mountaineers will frown at the thought of packing any "extras." The ethos of "light is right" really does increase safety by enabling the party to move faster, thus minimizing their time exposed to objective hazards. Think about the additional weight of any extras you're contemplating. That said, here are three extras that I normally carry: thin-closed cell foam pad—good for a seat at lunch and great for overnight insulation; collapsible ski poles—hike up faster, hike down safer, but stow them when climbing; helmet liner (even though I packed a wool hat)—warm and comfy.

A word on essential gear for safety
As stated at the beginning of this short section, listed here are only those items that could be different from those normally carried when hiking. In reality, there is more in a competent scrambler's pack than listed here. Texts, such as *Mountaineering: The Freedom of the Hills*, provide a list of what a person should carry in the mountains. If you've been hiking and backpacking for years, but haven't read it, it is worth your time to do so. If you aspire to greater climbs, it is the best book to start with and will fill in the many gaps I've skipped over.

Here's what's in my pack

This is what I take for a single-day, difficult and remote scramble in the cool Canadian Rockies autumn weather

Light-weight bivy bag
First-aid kit
Split
Headlamp with strobe
Camera tripod
Multi-tool
Satellite phone
Sunglasses (2)
Climbing watch
Stick of sunscreen
Harness

Map and compass
Rain jacket
Helmet
Windproof and insulated jacket
Fleece hat and gloves
Rope
Locking carabiners (2)
Belay device
Rappel tape
Trekking pole

If I'm expecting snow or ice, I'll include: ice ax, crampons and waterproof over mitts.

Scrambling skills

The physical skills required for safe and efficient scrambling need to be taught. Furthermore, your ability to adequately execute these skills for safe mountain travel should be critiqued and assessed. You may be a natural at climbing, however, time spent with a certified guide who enjoys teaching new climbers is definitely time and money well spent.

My hope for this book is that it encourages prospective scramblers to demand comprehensive training from competent sources. In doing so, I hope that at least one scrambling injury or death will be prevented. The Alpine Club of Canada has offered scrambling skills courses, but not all new scramblers have access to this kind of training, nor are most aware that it is available. In this regard, incidents that would have likely been prevented by scrambling education continue. If "scrambling-specific" training is not conveniently available to you, then I strongly suggest introductory mountaineering courses that cover the skills listed here.

Walk efficiently

- Always conserve your strength and pace your activity. If you discover yourself breathing heavily over a long period of time, you are probably pushing yourself too hard. Pace yourself. If you start out too fast, you will tire more quickly. A good rule is to plan short and, if necessary, frequent rest stops. If your breaks are too long, your body has a hard time getting going again.

- The way that you walk also has a lot to do with how much exertion and wear your body can tolerate in a day. When walking uphill, don't walk on your toes. It is a lot easier on your legs if you stretch your heels down to the ground. If you are going up a slope (off-trail) and find it difficult to keep your heels down, consider switchbacking at an indirect angle across slopes to lessen the angle of your ascent. Allowing your heels to rest on the ground greatly reduces the stress to your ankles and lower legs.

- When going downhill, keep your knees slightly bent. This disperses the stress of being pulled downhill onto your leg muscles, rather than your joints. Also try widening your stride to both sides. This disperses a portion of your momentum to the sides rather than all downhill.

Stepping up steep slopes

When not wearing crampons, there are two stepping techniques that scramblers can employ: the rest step and edging.

Rest step

The rest step is employed to conserve the climbing power of your quadriceps and can steady your breathing during long slogs or at higher elevations. At first, it may slow your pace a little, but once you establish a solid rhythm, you'll find that the steadiness gained will get you to the summit faster than an exhausting sprint-recover sequence. Lactic acid removal and cramping can both be aided by using the rest step. As soon as you find your pace starting to slow, fall into the rest step to maintain a steady pace. Note that the rest in the rest step is very short, so short that the person using the rest step displays a continuous motion. See pictures and caption below.

During the rest step your uphill knee moves as a hinge. Instead of flexing your quadriceps to move up, think of straightening your knee to stand tall. Lock the downhill knee when the leg is straight and feel your body weight move over the knee to be supported by the bones of the new downhill leg. Now rest for the smallest instant, then continue.

In the top photograph, the scrambler is giving a glancing kick to the slope. When the platform is made, the toe and heel are at the same height (bottom photograph).

Edging

Edging is something that many people unknowingly employ in order to stabilize foot placements on scree and snow. Edging is accomplished by digging the edge of your boot sole into the slope. Both outside and inside edges are employed alternatively. The key to effective edging is to keep your heel and toe at the same height. Once you become comfortable with committing your body weight to the edge of your boots, you can then move up or down the slope with as little as a centimetre of boot sole in contact with the mountain. Failing to keep the toe and heel at the same height, however, will likely result in a slip or fall. Refer to the edging photographs.

When the ground is frozen, but not yet covered with snow, you may have to kick many times to carve an adequate platform for effective edging. You can also use this technique when climbing harder snow without crampons. Kick into the slope with a "glancing arc" to form the platform.

Remember to put a good effort into edging. The scramblers following you will expect to only improve slightly on the edged steps you've created during your turn as trailbreaker.

Here, you can see the stable platform, about half the width of the boot, made by repeated kicks.

Typical Rockies scree encountered en route to many summits.

Be careful when crossing slabs covered with loose rock. The smaller rock will act as tiny ball bearings and slips are common. Photo: Dave Stephens

Managing loose rock

Scree

As scree gets smaller, travel normally gets easier until the rock size approaches that of pea gravel. Climbing in fine scree resembles hiking up a sand dune: it is both tiring and frustrating. For scree larger and more stable than sand, edging is effective where a beaten trail has not been cut. For upward progress, you can try step-kicking as you would in snow, however, it is less effective than edging and will accelerate wear on your boots. Step-kicking in scree will destroy plastic mountaineering boots. If you don't like climbing scree, you'll be frustrated by many of the scrambles in the Canadian Rockies. But, scree can be fun—especially on the way down! A good scree run can chop hours off an otherwise tedious descent. Plunge-stepping, however, is safer than an all-out run, although sometimes it's hard to hold yourself back. If you can plunge-step in snow, scree will be almost as easy.

Talus

Talus is basically a boulder field. Some talus is composed of rocks the size of your refrigerator and stable enough that weighting the rock on any exposed surface will not cause it to wobble, slide or roll. Hopping from rock to rock in these fields can quickly propel you across a relatively steep slope. Fields of smaller boulders, the size of your microwave oven, are more challenging and normally less stable. There is no real trick to moving through talus, and

Plunge-stepping down scree is a skill that needs to be learned and practiced. Photo: Sonny Bou.

it's critical that you exercise caution with respect to rock stability. Rocks or boulders that have been deposited hundreds or thousands of years ago are likely to be more stable than the more recently deposited ones. Shifting of the mountain and the freeze/thaw cycle allow these older rocks to settle into each other. A real danger exists on recently formed talus fields or new boulders thrown down on older fields. These rocks may be precariously balanced on some minor feature and just waiting for an inattentive scrambler to step on the rock sending it, and the scrambler, tumbling down the mountain. Remember, these boulders are big and can weigh several tonnes. It's possible for one to roll as you step on it and pin your leg between it and other boulders. You could require several strong rescuers to free your shattered leg ... or one calm surgeon to amputate.

You can recognize newly deposited rocks by looking for signs of recent scarring, a "fresh" cut or newly exposed surface. Talus covered with soil, grasses or trees is likely more stable since it takes many years for wind-deposited soil to accumulate. Even talus covered with tiny lichen is evidence of a long history of being detached from its mountain home. Find-

ing many newly deposited boulders should alert you to an extreme rockfall hazard. I climb certain mountains every year, and this year I noticed some new and large rocks deposited in the approach gullies. This tells me that the winter/spring thaw has been unusually erosive to the local peaks. Armed with this information, I add an extra measure of caution to my excursions.

Be aware that any of these boulders could roll when weighted. Crossing talus fields like this requires extra care.

The basics of movement on rock

The ability to efficiently climb 3rd- and 4th-class rock is the second most important skill scramblers require; the most important being the ability to exercise good judgment with respect to objective hazards. Efficient climbing is characterized by speed, confidence, energy conservation and not falling! All of us are born with a strong desire to climb and some climbing ability. Just spend some time watching children at a neighbourhood playground and you'll see joy in their faces when they finally make it to the top of the monkey bars or a favourite tree. Even if you haven't climbed anything in years, once you develop skill and confidence, that same childhood joy will be back.

Some exposure to rock or gym climbing will help a scrambler build skill in the mountains. But scramblers don't need to be rock climbers to safely summit. Scramblers do need to be taught, and then practice, the few critical climbing concepts that are relevant to scrambling. Once you've found a suitably qualified person to provide the climbing training required for scrambling, ensure that the following concepts are emphasized:

Footwork

Hands and feet must be placed in a manner that maximizes the friction between you and the rock. Third-class scrambling routes can normally be climbed with minimum reliance on handholds. Even when scramblers progress to 4th-class terrain, handholds are only used minimally for climbing and mostly for balance. The emphasis, therefore, of movement training for scrambling should be on footwork. Good climbers have great footwork.

Good footwork will enable you to rely on your larger leg muscles rather than your arms. Most new climbers tend to exert a death grip on the nearest or biggest handhold instead of focusing on setting up a strong foothold. Along with the

Remember, your goal is to move from one position of balance to another. Try to keep your hips in, your weight over your feet and use your hands for balance only—no death grips.

It takes time to scramble with confidence. This climber makes it look easy, but don't expect to look this relaxed until you've accumulated lots of experience. Photo: Sonny Bou.

power conservation that comes with good footwork, you'll also have better balance and confidence. Good balance is characterized by being able to comfortably stand in a position that transfers your body weight directly over your feet. Movement on rock is safest when the climber moves from one balanced position to the next balanced position. From strength and comfort comes confidence. Never forget, however, to temper newfound confidence with good judgment. If you're not careful, you may find yourself confidently climbing to a stranded position, where you can't find the next move up or down.

Three points of contact

The gymnastic movement of an accomplished rock climber working out a problem on a 5.13 bolted sport route has little in common with the movement of a scrambler high on a knife-edged ridge battling the wind and cold. On the sport route, the climber will attempt to employ advanced techniques that most would never risk on an alpine climb. The cost of failure in remote mountain ranges is too great. The concepts taught to new rock climbers, however, are invaluable to the scrambler. One of the primary lessons is to try to maintain three points of contact with the rock at all times. Those three points of contact are any combination of hands and feet. The concept of three points of contact is that you only move one limb at a time thus allowing

Move one limb at a time to maintain three points of contact at all times. Photo: Dave Stephens

Scrambling through 3rd-class terrain. Photo: Dave Stephens

three to remain on the rock. Once comfortably balanced using both feet and hands, you would then identify your next hold, evaluate its integrity (next section) then commit a foot or hand to it. One at a time. A good instructor will critique your movement on low-angled routes to ensure you practice three points of contact. The discipline you develop there will help you work confidently through tougher routes later. Speed comes with practice.

Evaluate before committing
Reading the section on rockfall in the chapter on objective hazards should alert you to an additional hazard encountered when climbing rotten rock: holds blow out and it is always a surprise. At least it should be a surprise if you have carefully tested each hold before committing your weight to it. Holds are tested from a position of balance by pulling, pounding or kicking them. If the hold is good, the only sound you should hear is the sound of your hand or boot hitting the rock. If the rock is loose, you should hear a hollow or knocking sound. A rubble heap of a mountain will likely have a rotten route to the summit. Vertical, or near-vertical, pitches of rotten rock present a hazard for all unroped climbing. If you commit to a hold before testing its integrity, then you are playing a game of Russian roulette: the next hold may be the one that blows.

Downclimbing

Maybe a house cat can risk climbing a tree and needing assistance to get down—whether it's the fire department, or a nice saucer of milk at the foot of the tree, "kitty" won't need to use one of his nine lives. Scramblers, however, do need to find a way down from where they have climbed. Generally, downclimbing is more difficult than upclimbing. Every year I hear local news reports of scramblers or hikers who required rescue from a ledge that they could not climb down from.

When you receive climbing instruction, make sure downclimbing is addressed. Even though it's harder than upclimbing, it is still safer than rappelling. Rappelling is a last resort for descending most scrambles. It's not that rappelling can't be done safely, it's the increased complexity due to the addition of gear and the vigilance required to check and double check all systems that increase the probability of human error. For most scramblers, downclimbing is the best option. Even though some scrambles require a rappel descent, rappelling is a mountaineering skill that is taught on an introductory mountaineering or rock-climbing course, not here.

Try to face out from the slope when downclimbing. This way, you can plot your route. However, if the angle is too steep, you may have to face in. Facing in is slower, but it is more secure.

The necessity to test each hold and move from one position of balance to the next holds true for downclimbing as well as going up. It's often said that good climbers look at their feet a lot. Strong foot placements are especially critical when moving down, because the tendency is to slightly unweight one foot as the other foot moves. If the stationary foothold blows in mid-move, all weight will shift to weaker arms.

Belaying the leader down a steep pitch. Photo: Andrew Nugara.

Both strong foot placements and maintaining weight on the stationary foot throughout a move will make for more secure downclimbing.

Beware of "easy" rock. *In 1988, two scramblers were descending a popular peak by way of some rock slabs that were not part of the normal descent route. One of them slipped and tumbled down the slabs, stopping just above a cliff. The falling scrambler suffered several cuts and bruises and needed to be slung out the next day.*

Tricky downclimbing on a 4th-class scramble. Facing out can give you the best view of the route, however, it is less secure than facing into the slope. Photo: Sonny Bou.

Steep grass

Off-trail travel across steep grassy slopes may be necessary in order to access a route. At first, it may seem odd to include, "walking on grass," in an introductory scrambling text, but I assure you that it has a place. Hikers and scramblers can be injured as a result of slips and falls on wet or snow-covered grassy slopes. These slopes are especially dangerous in the spring when the grass still lies flat from the weight of the winter's snow. Any moisture on these slopes will create a near-frictionless surface.

If you must travel this terrain, ensure that you will not cause undue environmental damage by tearing up the slope with the lug soles of your boots. It's always best to stay on a trail or route in order to lessen the damage to terrain. Travel across wet grassy slopes is best done with the assistance of trekking poles or an ice axe. In the most severe of conditions, you may even consider wearing crampons.

Bushwhacking

Bushwhacking is off-trail travel through dense vegetation. It is normally done to gain the base of a route that does not have a defined approach trail. It is frequently done inadvertently if scramblers lose an established approach trail and need to crash through the bush to, hopefully, find their original path.

Bushwhacking safety is likely known and practiced by experienced hikers, but the tips below merit inclusion.

Bushwhacking tips

- Beware of navigation errors when you lose distant terrain references in dense bush. It is prudent to keep to a compass bearing until you emerge from the thickets.
- Be alert to the possibility of abrupt terrain changes such as cliffs or gullies
- The vegetation at your feet might be so dense that you are unable to determine whether you are walking on the ground or suspended above it by the stout undergrowth. If this is the case, beware of sudden changes in the vegetation's density that can result in an ankle-twisting drop.
- Keep your group together so no one becomes disoriented or lost
- Make noise to warn any aggressive animals of your presence
- Take your time. You can waste a lot of energy in frustrated floundering.

When in doubt, rope-up. It only takes a minute or two.

Belaying

Scramblers should learn basic belay techniques. Belay is the term used to describe a safety system that is employed to minimize the consequences of a fall. There are three categories of belay: self-belay, belaying a second and belaying a leader. The self-belay is a technique used for movement over snow. Belaying a lead scrambler is normally only required on the most difficult scrambling routes or on routes that are plagued with the worst of conditions. I feel that these techniques should best be learned by scramblers who wish to progress to climbing 5th-class routes.

Belaying your companions

Scrambling parties commonly consist of climbers of varying skill. Sometimes one climber may be competent and comfortable enough to climb through a difficult pitch that other members of the party can't climb. If, after the difficult pitch (crux), the route eases to a level that the weaker climbers could continue, then the leader can belay the others up through the crux. On the way down from the summit, the better climber will likely have to belay the others down the crux, and then downclimb unroped. Remember to never climb up a pitch that you are not positive you can downclimb.

A typical view from a solid sitting belay.

Instruction techniques may vary, however, the elements of the belay do not. Every belay needs a belay position, an anchor, a rope, a method to apply friction to the rope and communication between the belayer and the climber.

A rear view of a solid sitting belay position. Note the well braced feet against the rock.

Sometimes, the best belay position may be to straddle a ridge.

Belay position

Choosing a position from which to belay is the first decision to make. Depending on the difficulty and length of the pitch, you could be belaying for half-an-hour or more. It's important to pick a comfortable location and the appropriate stance to take in that location. On scrambling routes, a comfortable spot for a sitting belay can usually be located easily. Once you've found the location and decided which stance to use, then you need to find an anchor.

Belay anchor

The anchor in the belay system is employed to secure the belayer to the slope so that the force applied to the system by a falling scrambler will not pull the belayer from the mountain. In this way, it actually protects both the belayer and the second. The construction of the anchor is dependent upon the direction and magnitude of the potential force of a second's fall, the terrain, the available equipment and the weight difference between the climber and the belayer. Recall that one of the differences between scrambling and rock climbing is that a roped fall would not leave the scrambler dangling. What this means is that the forces on the belay system from a scrambling fall or slip should be significantly less than in rock or ice climbing. This fact does not negate the requirement for an anchor, but it does influence the type of anchor employed.

At the very minimum, an anchor can simply be the belayer securely braced against a rock, thereby using only the terrain, their weight and strength to protect the climber. Ensure that the direction of pull is factored into the construction of every anchor or stance. This system would provide protection for falls or slips that apply minimum forces to the system. But another scenario may demand that the belayer use a system of cord and slings secured to both their climbing harness and some natural feature. This belay would protect falls that apply greater forces to the system; however,

What makes a good belay position

- It should be comfortable
- The terrain features should facilitate a strongly braced stance
- Look for terrain, such as a rock horn or large tree trunk, that can be positioned between the belayer's legs
- Look for a position where the belayer can sit in a "bucket" where any force generated by the climber will not pull the belayer free of the belay
- The position should be solid so that any movement of the rope or belayer will not knock loose rock on the climber

since the consequences of failure are such that both belayer and climber could be pulled from the mountain, scramblers must seek instruction and practice in order to construct this system correctly. Scramblers should avoid routes that require this type of belay, referred to as a 5th-class belay, because the greater the forces applied to the belay, the greater the possibility that the belay may fail.

Two views of the same standing belay. This scrambler is using the terrain as a brake.

The rope

The climber and belayer are joined by the belay rope. A good scrambling rope only needs to be 25 m to 35 m long and 8.5 mm to 9 mm in diameter. While these thin ropes are light, thicker ropes are easier to grip. The rope does not need to be water resistant (so-called dry ropes). Since the forces applied to the rope from a fall on 3rd- or 4th-class routes are only a fraction of those 5th-class routes, the diameter of the rope may be smaller and the tested number of falls can be lower. Thirty metres of scrambling rope is cheaper than a good harness or a helmet. Take care of your rope and inspect it after every scramble and after a significant force has been applied to it.

Rock will abrade the rope, thereby shortening its life. Be very careful to never load the rope if the rope is passing over any sharp-edged rocks. Do not be persuaded to use someone's retired climbing rope. You need to know the history of all safety equipment. You'll need to learn a few knots. At the very minimum, every climber should be able to tie an overhand knot, an overhand on a bight, figure 8, figure 8 on a bight, double fishermen's knot, water knot, prusik hitch and a Münter hitch. This may sound like

A good sticky terrain brake.

a lot of knots, but if you're going to use safety systems that employ ropes, slings and cord, you'll need these knots. Knots should be taught on a scrambling skills course. You can also read one of the standard mountaineering texts, or one of several knot books. Buy three metres of 8 mm climbing rope, then practice. You'll be amazed how quickly you can learn to tie climbing knots. If you learn to tie them before your course, you'll be able to spend more time on other skills.

Using a Black Diamond ATC belay device.

Belaying a leader

The most common scrambling scenario requiring a leader belayed is where the leader is starting up from an extremely exposed position; an example being two scramblers on a ledge above a significant drop where the route continues above the ledge. If the leader fell from this position, he might fall past the ledge and into the abyss. In this situation, the leader can be belayed by the anchored second. Then, if the leader fell, he would only fall a rope length below the belay. This is known as a factor-2 fall, and it is much better than a free fall to the ground. Unprotected climbing, in this situation, is risky and should really be considered soloing. Since the topic of this book is safer scrambling techniques, I recommend scramblers consistently avoid any route where a leader would normally require a belay, either due to technical difficulty or exposure.

Here, the leader is belayed due to the cliff behind the second. If the leader fell past the second, the belay should arrest the fall. In this photographs, the second has just removed a terrain brake.

Applying friction

Once again, due to the lower forces applied to the belay during a scrambling fall, scramblers have the luxury of being able to employ techniques that are seldom used in a modern 5th-class belay. There are three basic methods to apply friction to the rope: using your body, using the terrain or using a belay device. Applying friction is often termed as applying a "brake." The brake hand must never leave the rope—never!

Applying friction to the rope by employing your body is done when using a hip belay or standing belay. Standing belays are seldom used in alpine or rock climbing, but are perfectly sound choices for some scrambling situations. In a hip belay, the belayer is sitting and wraps the rope about two-thirds around his hips. To apply a brake, the belayer simply completes the final third of the wrap, thus applying increased friction.

The rope in the left hand is called the live end; the belayed scrambler is attached to this end. The rope in the right hand is called the brake. The belayer will pull slack with her left hand so the rope will be slid across her back bringing her right hand forward and her left hand back towards her body.

She then slides her left hand forward past the right one. Once the left hand is just in front of the right, the left hand grasps both ropes.

Then, without letting go of the brake end, the scrambler loosens her grip on the brake and slides her right hand back to a position where she can begin to take-in the slack again.

Letting go of the brake rope with the left hand brings her back to the start position shown here and in the first photograph.

To apply the brake, the scrambler simply completes the wrap around her body.

Because it's difficult to apply an effective brake to a standing belay, it is only used to aid a scrambler over a pitch where a slip would apply only the very minimum of force on the belayer. I only use a standing belay to "short rope" a climber up a particularly low angle but slippery slope. I also only use it to help climbers who are much lighter than me. It's critical to keep all the slack out of the system in order to minimize the forces if the climber should slip. Avoid using standing belays on snow or ice and when the belayer may be inclined toward the climber.

Another method of applying friction to the system that can be employed by a scrambler, but seldom by a rock or alpine climber, is to use available terrain: the theory being that any increased force on the system will cause the rope to bind against the terrain or be wedged into a constriction. While the climber is moving up and making progress, the belayer must be able to keep slack out of the system. This can be difficult on the lower angled terrain common to scrambling as the rope will tend to grab the rock. Ensure that the terrain brake is only "activated" when the climber exerts force on the system and not when the belayer is taking in the slack.

In choosing a piece of terrain for braking friction, make sure that it's not too sharp or loose. Most terrain belays will employ large boulders or a ridge as the terrain brake. During scrambling courses, instructors can demonstrate the amazingly heavy loads that the mere friction of the rope pressed against a rock can support. Terrain brakes are especially handy when you can't find a comfortable place to sit or stand and really need to rely on a brake instead of a stance.

Finally, the most effective method of applying friction to a rope is the belay device. Belay devices come in many shapes. In keeping with the "light is right" philosophy, pick a small device that will accommodate the diameter of rope you use. Simple devices are best. Try a few before you buy. Devices used in climbing gyms, such as Grigri's, are completely unsuited for scrambling; they're just too heavy and bulky. Proper set-up and use of a belay device, locking carabineer and harness, like all climbing skills, is best learned under the watchful eye of a pro. Make sure that you always incorporate a rock-solid stance when using any belay device. The belay device only applies friction to the rope. It does not secure you to the mountain.

Fifth-class belays require training, practice and vigilance. *In 1997, two climbers were reported as overdue by a friend. Their bodies were found at the base of a moderate rock climb located in the Bow Valley of Alberta. Investigators believe that the force of a leader fall tore out the anchor, causing both the leader and belayer to fall to their deaths.*

Natural protection

Natural protection is the employment of natural features, such as vegetation and various rock features as the primary attachment point for a sling or length of cord. The sling or cord is then attached to the rope with a carabineer. Alternatively, the climbing rope may simply be looped around or weaved through the feature. Features that can serve as natural protection are tree trunks, roots, branches, rock horns, flakes and various constrictions or tunnels. All these feature must be evaluated before your life, and that of your climbing partner, are committed to them. If it's strong enough to hang your car from, it's likely strong enough to clip.

Some readers may choose to learn and practice scrambling skills without the assistance of a certified guide. Although I do not recommend this practice, I know it will happen ... perhaps it will be the path of the majority. Throughout this book, I have recommended professional instruction more strongly for certain skills such as belay technique, travel over glaciated terrain and avalanche assessment. The construction of natural protection is another skill that, truly, should be taught by a certified guide. Please heed this advice.

While a scrambling skills course may include some instruction on the employment of natural protection, don't be surprised if your guide suggests that you gain more climbing experience before you attempt to use these techniques. You would likely only need to employ them on difficult 4th-class terrain and higher. Don't climb these routes until you're ready.

Typical snowfield found at the summit of many Rockies peaks. Photo: Dave Stephens

Movement on snow

The avalanche potential must be assessed before any travel on snow. There are excellent texts available, however, you may learn more from an avalanche awareness course. They're offered in most mountain communities and by outdoor education providers. Once you've assessed the avalanche risk and have determined that safe travel is possible, then determine how the snow will influence your progress: will it speed you up or slow you down? Some snow is hard, making it easy to travel over terrain that might impede your travel if the ground were bare, such as over talus or scree. Some snow is as slippery as ice and some will not support your weight, thereby forcing you to grunt through it and plow a nice trench for others to follow.

Scrambling routes are normally out of condition when there is any accumulation of snow, making the route a true alpine climb rather than a scramble. In the Canadian Rockies, most routes start to come into condition in June. On the other hand, some are not ready until August or might never be free enough of snow until the next warm summer! When routes are in condition, scramblers typically encounter snow a few metres from the summit or in a shaded aspect. Some routes require a short traverse across a shallow and low-angled snowfield that didn't manage to fully melt in the spring. Most of these conditions can be easily managed with careful attention to foot placement, a couple of climbing techniques and an ice axe. Crampons are great, but most minor snow features can be negotiated in boots alone.

If you're ascending straight up the slope, try to angle your steps downward for a more secure purchase. If you're going up diagonally, still try to angle the steps slightly downward, but also remember to keep your toe and heel at the same height.

Post-holing is the mountaineering term for the exhausting exercise of walking through snow that does not support your weight. You'll create nice round holes of varying depth created by each frustrating step. The leader will suffer the most. But followers will find the travel nearly as tiring. Gaiters are a must and snow-shedding pants are helpful, as long as you won't overheat in either of them. If the snow is such that you aren't able to walk or hike through it, either because it's too hard or too steep, then two stepping techniques can be useful.

Step-kicking

Step-kicking is a team sport. The leader may create the steps, but the following members of the party will improve them. The trailing scrambler will enjoy the good work of their teammates as they climb on sturdy, well-sculpted steps. The type of ascent, either direct or diagonal, will determine the technique.

For a direct ascent, face into the slope and kick directing in with the toe of your boot. Your objective is to create steps that are shoulder width apart and will support your weight. The depth of the step will be determined by how hard you kick and the relative hardness of the snow. The deeper the step, the more weight it will support. However, don't kick deeper than the first half of your foot; steps that are shin-deep are awkward to climb. Trying to keep the angle of the platform slightly downward as the boot goes into the slope will make the step more secure. Keep the vertical distance between the steps manageable by all members of your party: shorter legs require shorter steps. To conserve your energy, let the weight of your boot swing around a relaxed knee. Nevertheless, if this method yields minimal penetration, you'll need to get aggressive. The vertical slopes you attempt as a scrambler should be relatively short; any long pitches of near vertical snow will change a scramble to an alpine climb.

If the ascent is diagonal, then kick steps parallel to the slope. Step-kicking for a traverse or a diagonal ascent is more difficult to accurately explain without an accompanying demonstration, however, the concept is the same: create platforms that will support your weight and assist the climbers following. Instead of kicking directly into the slope, as in a direct ascent (described above), kick parallel to the slope and create a step that supports the entire length of your boot's edge—toe to heel. The depth of the step, in this case, is measured from the slope to the boot edge furthest from the slope—just like edging on scree. Again, trying to keep the angle of the step slightly downward as it enters the slope will make it more secure.

Lastly, creating effective steps requires cooperative snow; the consistency must be such that steps can be formed. Steps are difficult to build in snow that is too loose or powdery. In these conditions, you can try to build steps by stamping the snow and compacting it underfoot. Again, these steps can be improved by the members of your party following behind you.

When plunge-stepping, stay in control, keep your knees slightly bent and your toes up. Photo: Bob Spirko.

Plunge-stepping

Plunge-stepping is a deliberate and vigorous technique used to directly descend steep slopes—either snow or scree. Like most techniques of movement used in mountaineering, it is best taught by demonstration.

I have listed only the very minimum of points to aid the new scrambler.

When plunge-stepping

- Keep your forward, weighted leg, slightly bent at the knee
- Keep your toes up and plunge with your heel
- Look forward and not down at your feet
- Control your speed and be able to stop at any time, but don't be timid in your technique
- Keep your ice axe in line with your leading foot and be ready to self arrest

Glissading

Glissading is the mountaineering term for a deliberate slide down a snow slope. Never attempt this on ice; the acceleration can be fatal. Most mountaineers glissade in order to descend a slope faster than if they were to plunge-step their way down. It may sound like a simple skill, however, it really should be taught by a professional since its finer points, like using your ice axe as a rudder, take some practice.

When glissading

- Never wear crampons. If you catch a point, you'll likely break an ankle.
- Beware of rocks or other dangerous debris in your path that can be hidden below the surface of the snow
- Choose the most stable position for the terrain. Sitting is not always best. Standing allows you to perform turns as if you were skiing.
- Make sure you are able to stop or slow down at any time: you may have misjudged the run-out or may need to assist a member of your party. Always be in control.
- Like downclimbing is normally safer than rappelling, plunge-stepping in normally safer than glissading

A fast way to descend providing you are under control and can stop at any time.
Photo: Sonny Bou.

This is not scrambling terrain. Glacier travel and crevasse rescue skills are required here.

Glaciers

The mass, movement and beauty of glaciers is awesome to behold. Glaciers exert their power to sculpt the landscape and even influence local weather. Gravity induces incredible forces of compression and strain that cause glaciers to move, change shape and fracture. Movement may be less than a few inches per day, but the results, crevasses and icefall, are some of the mountaineer's greatest objective hazards. Route finding through glaciated terrain, especially a jumbled icefall or a heavily crevassed aspect, requires all the technical skills of basic glacier travel and a good deal of mountain experience.

A discussion about glacier travel and crevasse rescue really has no place in a book on scrambling. I've crossed glaciers on the approach to scramble routes, and I've also taken the time to learn and practice the requisite skills to cross glaciers safely and perform self-rescue, if necessary. If you'd ask me if I felt that outing was a scramble, I'd say, "No, it was an easy alpine climb."

Most of the terrain in any mountain range can be access by hiking or scrambling. If you learn to manage the objective hazards and gently increase your experience, you can likely spend a lifetime scrambling in your local range without ever having to cross crevassed glaciers. If you do want to tackle scrambles that require crossing glaciers, either take a course from a certified guide or go with an experienced group.

Routefinding and navigation

The ability to navigate using only a map and compass is more than practical, it's empowering. One of the remnants of my years in the military is the ability to confidently rely on a map and compass to navigate unfamiliar terrain. Navigation in most mountainous regions of North America is fairly straightforward, but it does require some competency with a map and compass: following ridges or valleys, climbing a peak to get oriented to the terrain and remembering that water flows downhill will all help. Being able to pinpoint your location on a map will give you a perspective of the neighbouring terrain that you can't appreciate from the ground.

Routefinding is the ability to assess the features of a mountain (ridges, gullies, ledges, snow fields, etc.), then link those features to create a climbable route to the summit. It is also the ability to recognize an existing route described in a guidebook, and then travel that same route to the summit.

Hikers new to scrambling should first test their routefinding ability by trying to recognize and travel existing routes before they attempt to formulate their own. This routefinding experience will build the skill necessary to chart your own safe routes to the summit. As you travel in the footsteps of others, you'll likely begin to notice that routes within one range tend to

Don't be tempted into a quick descent via an unknown gully.
Exit gullies like this one can often hide dangerous cliff bands. Photo: Dave Stephens.

Scramblers must be able to judge their rock climbing ability when trying to find a route up a complex peak such as Dolomite Peak in the Canadian Rockies. While there are several possible routes to the summit, only one is easy enough for 4th-class climbers. Photo Sonny Bou.

follow similar features. For example, most Canadian Rockies' routes tend to follow dominant gullies.

Don't climb yourself into a trap; whether on route or off. *A lone scrambler climbed a complex route up a popular peak in Banff National Park in 1989. He attempted to retrace his route upon descent. However, he downclimbed himself into unknown territory and became stranded on a ledge. Unable to climb up or down from his final position, he spent two nights alone before being rescued by park wardens.*

Routefinding tips

- When looking up at a slope, it appears steeper than is truly is
- When looking down a slope, it appears less steep than it is
- Always choose your descent route before you start the scramble. Then reassess it before you start down.
- Beware of hidden cliff bands on new descent routes
- Try to avoid long traverses. A direct ascent is more efficient.
- Don't expect to ascend a new route as quickly as a familiar route.
- Generally, more solid rock can be found on ridges where there is also less danger from rockfall

Navigating in a whiteout

Being in a whiteout has been described as being trapped inside of a ping-pong ball. Typically, strong winds will suspend fine snow crystals such that all landmarks are lost in a dull, grey nightmare. While cross-country skiing near Winnipeg, Manitoba, I've been caught in whiteouts so severe that I could barely see the tips of my skis!

Whiteouts can form in all mountain terrain in the winter, of course, and on any large expanse of snow during the rest of the year. The ice fields between Lake Louise and Jasper, Alberta, are prime whiteout terrain in any season.

Navigation and route finding in a whiteout requires you to practice the skills necessary for any mountain travel experience: know where you are and know where you want to be. If you can find these two places on your map or GPS, then it's just a matter of getting there. But getting there in a whiteout can be difficult and dangerous. Scramblers really shouldn't find themselves in whiteout-prone terrain. These areas are the realm of the trained mountaineer. Scramblers venturing into the high mountains above snowline should be prepared to wait out whiteout conditions, or be equipped and have enough experience to travel through it. They should have a whiteout navigation plan, and stick to it.

Remember to stay away from whiteout-prone terrain. But if you find yourself caught in a whiteout, here are a few basics tips for whiteout navigation.

Whiteout navigation

- If you can maintain a compass bearing, and there are no obstacles en route, travel in a straight line to your final destination
- Sometimes it may be easier to travel, in a straight line, between known points such as peaks, ridges, cols, etc. Link these points together to get to your final destination.
- Instead of straight compass bearings, you may be able to follow a known ridge or valley
- Knowing the elevation of known points or your destination will enable you to use an altimeter as a navigation tool
- Learn map skills like plotting grid references and measuring distance
- Remember that travelling in whiteout conditions will take longer than normal

Dealing with emergencies

All backcountry travellers should be able to extricate themselves from the wilderness if they find themselves off route or overdue. The capability to survive a night out, and suffer through the discomfort, is the mark of an experienced scrambler. The term "stranded," with respect to scrambling, typically means that scramblers have climbed to a position from which they cannot climb up or down. From this position, they will either need to be rescued or talked down. "Overdue" means that you are able to make it back to the trailhead, but it will take you longer than expected. "Lost" is a temporary condition that will come to an end in one of three ways: you'll find your own way back, you'll be found by searchers, or you'll die.

Stranded

To avoid becoming stranded, scramblers should only commit themselves to routes which they can downclimb or rappel. In order to follow this guideline, vigilance is required throughout the climb; you must constantly assess your position to ensure you can retreat. On difficult routes, it can be a comfort to be belayed down a crux by a leader who can then rappel. Normally, a 30 m short-rope and a couple of long slings will be all that is needed. On some occasions, a full-length climbing rope and a few pitons may be required. Try to avoid routes that require hardware to facilitate a retreat until you have mastered the skills required to place artificial protection. (Rock protection, harnesses, etc., require some advanced mountaineering skills. Please seek qualified instruction first.)

Scramblers might also become stranded and require assistance if weather conditions change in mid-route, thereby making retreat too dangerous. Again, this can be avoided by studying weather reports before you leave home and paying attention to the sky as you climb. Even though you are travelling light, if you are caught out in bad weather, you should have enough kit in your pack to survive and make it down when the weather lifts.

Overdue

Being overdue, basically being late with no other consequences, is not necessarily dangerous, however, it can initiate a rescue. Be realistic regarding your return time when you register with the local parks or public safety office prior to your climb. If you are running behind, try to call someone on your cellular or satellite phone and provide them with an updated plan. If you are on a multi-day excursion, you should be prepared for small changes to the schedule by packing extra food and fuel. On these longer trips, you may not want rescue efforts launched until some time has elapsed; 48 hours for example. If you're based from a tent or have left a vehicle parked at a trailhead, leave a note that details your schedule. Don't forget to remove the note upon your return. Clearly, some form of communication is ideal in any overdue situation.

Lost

Unlike wilderness mountaineering or extended-range backpacking trips, it's uncommon to get lost on a scramble. (Going off-route isn't really like being lost.) Additionally, you can focus on staying found throughout your scramble by doing what follows. There has been excellent research carried out on how people become lost—check out the reference list. One concept worthy of study is that of the "mental map."

If you read a scrambling route description in a guidebook, thumb through the associated hiking guide to review the approach, and finally, study a topographical map. This will help you imprint a mental map in your brain that has been derived from all the references you've disseminated. But this new mental map is purely perception and imagination—regardless of its accuracy. The accuracy of the mental map will only be validated as you travel the trail and route. This validation process is the primary activity that will determine whether you become lost or not. During this validation, you are receiving feedback from the environment that will either support or discredit your mental map. Feedback is continuous, so it must be evaluated continually. A piece of information that had supported your mental map may, after assessing new information, cast the mental map in doubt.

In order to further clarify the concept of mental map validation, try this exercise: read the description of a popular hiking trail that you have never travelled. Study the trail description and visualize twist, turns, terrain and scenery as described in the guide. As soon as possible after the visualization, go hike the trail. Do not take a map or guidebook (make sure it's a popular trail in great condition with minimal objective hazards). With every step and turn, compare your experience to the mental map you formed earlier. Try to list the items within your mental map that have changed because of your experience. Also list the features of the terrain that support your initial mental map and those that do not correlate. Your final objective is to change your mental map. At the end of a successful hike—not getting lost—your mental map is 100 per cent accurate.

This exercise may not sound all that relevant to climbing a complex scrambling route where all the gullies and ridges look the same—but it is. With every step on any route, keep updating your mental map with reality: reality is the terrain at your feet. By doing this you will be letting go of perception and imagination and replacing both with facts. Making route decisions based on false perceptions and imagination is how people become lost. Accept where you are going and update your map accordingly.

So you're lost

Now, if you do become lost, appreciating that being lost is truly a temporary condition is the first step toward controlling the lost traveller's worst enemy: panic. Secondly, if you have failed to find your way back to the route or trail, but you have prepared for your excursion as suggested in this book, you should be confident that your designated responsible person will notify the appropriate agency once you are suitably overdue. Finally, since you have also packed and prepared to gently suffer through a character-building night in the hills, you need only to sit tight and wait for rescue or navigational inspiration.

Tips for handling being lost

- Focus on staying alive and trying to help aprehensive companions
- Avoid travelling at night
- Small parties should stay together
- Large parties of eight or more can split into sub-groups of four. Four people are the optimum minimum party size (if one climber gets injured then two can go for help while one stays with the injured climber).
- Keep hydrated, fed, warm and dry
- Focus on topography rather than finding the trail. For example, if you are confident that you can safely descend a valley to a river that intersected a road, it really doesn't matter whether or not you walk on the trail—just get to the road.
- Avoid becoming lost a second time by becoming familiar with your new surroundings. Establish a reference point or a "home plate." As you explore, always know how to get back to your reference point.
- Conserve your energy. Don't overextend yourself when lost—you're just asking for panic. Climbers have survived many days of fasting and minimal hydration, by choice, in order to make the summit! You are likely very close to the route out. Stay calm. Relax and work smarter, not harder.

Medical emergencies

While major medical problems such as heart attacks and strokes are rare among fit scramblers, most people who scramble in the mountains will become involved, directly or indirectly, in injury accidents if they pursue their sport long enough.

Frequent scramblers should, at the very minimum take a basic first-aid course. The knowledge and skills necessary to recognize the signs and symptoms of common injuries and provide treatment, will not only provide comfort to your casualty, but will serve to trigger positive actions that will inhibit the escalation of the incident.

The possibility of injury accidents is not the only reason for acquiring a knowledge of first aid. Often it's the minor problems that, left unresolved, lead to potentially life-threatening situations. For example, the onset of heat exhaustion may lead to a lapse in concentration which precedes a slip and fall.

Basic first aid does not adequately impart the knowledge of human anatomy, physiology, casualty assessment, diagnosis and decision-making skills necessary to respond to more severe medical problems. Deep in the mountains you may not be able to secure medical advice over a radio or cell phone.

If you become a serious scrambler you should consider taking a wilderness first-aid course—many injuries and minor illnesses can be managed in the field by moderately trained lay people. These in-depth courses are specifically designed to help people deal with emergencies in a wilderness setting where help may be hours or days away.

In most mountain communities there are opportunities to advance your training in emergency medical response. While the cost of wilderness first-aid courses offered by public and private institutions can be significant relative to the cost of a new pair of boots or a GPS, the cost becomes insignificant if a life is saved. Take the time to read the first-aid section in the books listed on page 110.

Solar injuries

Experienced mountain hikers should already understand the dangers of excessive exposure to ultraviolet radiation. Therefore, only a few key facts require mentioning here.

UVB is the wavelength of light most harmful to skin and makes up only about 2 per cent of the total UV radiation. As you climb higher, there is less atmosphere available to filter and scatter sunlight. In fact, skin-burning radiation increases about 4 per cent with every 300 m (1,000 ft) climbed. At 3000 m (10,000 ft) there's about 50 per cent more radiation present than at sea level. If you find yourself in a snow-filled bowl or couloir, up to three-quarters of the incident solar energy can be reflected onto you by the snow —that's 175 per cent of the incident energy!

If a scrambler spends a significant amount of time—over fifteen to twenty minutes—travelling over snow, some extra precautions should be taken. Lather sunscreen on exposed skin, put sun block on your ears, nose and lips. Ensure that sunscreen makes it to the underside of the chin and nose: some climbers have found that the inside of their nose will become sunburnt after spending a day on a glacier. Wear sunglasses even on cloudy days, as atmospheric scattering of solar radiation will contribute to increased burning. Sunglasses that are not too dark, but provide UVB protection, are great for cloudy days or at dawn and dusk (carry two pairs of glasses in case one is lost or damaged).

One more potential ailment of excessive solar radiation is snow blindness, which results from solar damage to the cornea. It's a temporary, but painful, condition and may not develop until some time after exposure. Once again, this danger can be avoided by wearing UV-filtering eyewear designed for outdoor sports. If you've lost or damaged both your sunglasses and need to travel over a sunny snowfield, you can improvise a pair of sunglasses by cutting narrow slits or poking holes in a piece of cardboard or plastic with a pin or knife.

Solar Injuries

- Because of reduced atmosphere at elevation, the danger posed by solar radiation increases as you climb
- You will not feel the effects of snow-blindness until after exposure to excessive radiation, therefore, you need to take preventative measures on any snow-covered terrain
- Make sure you pack your sunglasses and a hat or visor

If you need to be rescued

Self-rescue

In the event of an emergency, the first thing you need to consider is whether you can handle it yourself. Can you effect a self-rescue? The capability to judge whether or not you can self-rescue, will come with experience. If in doubt, call for help. If you live through an "unnecessary" rescue, you will have the opportunity to thank your rescuers, apologize and ensure it doesn't happen again.

Calling for help

Public safety personnel use several criteria to determine when a rescue is necessary and how it will be executed. Do not expect to be rescued immediately, especially if you have called late in the day. Most rescues in remote areas rely on helicopters to transport the rescuers to the area and often to sling you off the mountain below the helicopter. This requires ample light and reasonable weather. If rescuers know your exact location, they may send in a party on foot to administer first-aid, provide warm clothes or sleeping bags and keep you company overnight.

Tips on rescue and self-rescue

- The capability and availability of backcountry rescue services varies greatly from region to region. Learn what's available for your climbing area and adjust your objectives accordingly.
- If the option is available, register your scramble with the local public safety office. (Sign out when you're finished!)
- Any attempt at self-rescue should start with actions that reduce risk. Never take-on increased risk, such as a dangerous rappel off a questionable anchor, in any self-rescue scenario.
- If you decide to attempt self-rescue, it is prudent to first notify the public safety office of your plan. They may be able to increase the safety of your attempt by providing information on the terrain, weather, etc. They may have a warden in the area who can provide assistance.
- In some areas, rescue can be initiated very quickly. Don't waste all your daylight trying to self-rescue or trying to decide whether or not to call for help.
- Always inform a responsible person of your trip and provide them with rescue instructions and contact information

Helicopter procedures

Nowadays helicopters are frequently used to rescue people in trouble in the mountains, often by slinging them out at the end of a cable. If you have to be rescued by helicopter, or are assisting in a rescue, a little knowledge about these aircraft and their operation can go a long way to ensuring everyone's safety.

- Before the chopper arrives, think about what needs to be done to ensure your own personal safety and the safety of those coming in to effect the rescue
- The landing zone should be 40 m (125 ft) in diameter
- Bare ground, such as a grassy meadow is the best landing site
- If the ground is snow-covered, try to colour it with juice crystals or mud, not loose items such as clothing or tree branches
- Helicopters cannot land on steep terrain. Find a fairly level location
- A strong draft is created by the rotors during landing and take-off. Ensure all loose items are packed or secured.
- Position yourself outside of the landing zone and stay there unless you are directed to approach the aircraft by the pilot or a crew member
- Beware of the tail rotor at all times. It rotates so quickly that it becomes invisible
- Changing winds on the ground can cause the main rotor blades to bend to within 4 feet of the ground. If you are directed to approach the aircraft while the main rotors are spinning, keep low, remove any loose headwear and tie long hair or tuck it away
- Always approach the aircraft from the front so the pilot can see you
- Obey all instructions
- If a sling extraction is necessary, obey all instructions from the rescue personnel, relax and enjoy the ride

Getting good instruction

If you've read this book in its entirety, you have, no doubt, identified three themes: scrambling can be dangerous, get instruction and get it from a certified guide. After this book is available for purchase, I'm not sure how I'll react to the next scrambling fatality. I know that previous injuries and fatalities prompted me to write this book, but what will I do as they continue? My only hope is that this book makes scrambling safer for you. However, simply reading about scrambling skills is not enough. You need to be taught some basic skills by a qualified instructor or guide. Furthermore, your ability to demonstrate those skills should be evaluated and critiqued.

If you can afford a pair of boots and a pack, you should be able to afford a scrambling skills course. You may be able to reduce the cost by teaming-up with a few friends and splitting the cost of a certified guide for a private one-day course. I believe that heading out with experienced friends or a group from a local club, without seeking qualified instruction first, is the wrong way to start.

A guide certified by the Association of Canadian Mountain Guides, or its equivalent, can teach you all the skills I have listed and provide the expertise and experience that can truly contribute to your safety better than any book could ever do. But don't forget that guides are people, too. Get a recommendation from a fellow scrambler or local club. There are several mountaineering schools that employ certified guides. Ensure your guide is properly certified. Outside of Canada's national parks, anyone can call themselves a "guide." If you have any concerns regarding the credentials of your guide, check out: www.acmg.ca.

References

The American Alpine Club and The Alpine Club of Canada. *Accidents in North American Mountaineering* in 2002, 2003 and 2004. Golden: The American Alpine Club, 2002, 2003, 2004.

Brighton, Patrick. *Climbers Guide for Treating Medical Emergencies*. Globe Pequot Press.

Bruce D., Md. Browne. Ed. *Emergency Care and Transportation of the Sick and Injured.* Jones and Bartlett, 2002

Burroughs, William. *Mountain Weather: A Guide for Skiers and Hillwalkers.* Marlborough, Wiltshire: The Crowood Press, 1995.

Cox, Steven M. and Kris Fulsaas, Eds. *Mountaineering: The Freedom of the Hills*, 7th Edition. Seattle: The Mountaineers Books, 2003.

Daffern, Tony. *Avalanche Safety for Skiers, Climbers and Snowboarders*, Calgary: Rocky Mountain Books, 1999.

Gonzales, Laurence. *Deep Survival: Who Lives, Who Dies and Why.* New York: Norton, 2003.

Houston, Mark, and Kathy Cosley. *Alpine Climbing: Techniques to take you higher.* Seattle: The Mountaineers Books, 2004.

Kane, Alan. *Scrambles in the Canadian Rockies*, new edition. Calgary: Rocky Mountain Books, 1999.

Letham, Lawrence. *GPS Made Easy*, 4th Edition. Calgary: Rocky Mountain Books, 2003.

Long, John. *How to Rock Climb: Climbing Anchors*, new ed. Globe Pequot Press. 2005.

Lourens, Tony. *Guide to Climbing.* Mechanicsburg: Stackpole Books, 2005.

McConnell, Bob. *Gentle Expeditions*. American Alpine Club Press. Seattle: The Mountaineers Books.

Paulcke, Wilhelm. *Hazards in Mountaineering*. Oxford: Oxford University Press, 1973.

Plotkin, Stuart. *The Hiking Engine: A Guide to the Care and Maintenance of Feet and Legs*. Birmingham: Menasha Ridge Press.

Powers, Phil. *Wilderness Mountaineering*. Mechanicsburg: Stackpole Books, 2000.

Raleigh, Duane. *Knots & Ropes for Climbers*. Mechanicsburg: Stackpole Books, 1998.

Twight, Mark F. *Extreme Alpinism: Climbing Light, Fast and High*. Seattle: The Mountaineers Books, 1999.

Viesturs, Ed. *Himalayan Quest: Ed Viesturs on the 8,000-Meter Giants*. Washington: The National Geographic Society, 2003.

Weiss, Eric A. *Wilderness 911. A Step-by-Step Guide for Medical Emergencies and Improvised Care in the Backcountry*. Seattle: The Mountaineers Books, 1998.

Wells, Darran. *NOLS Wilderness Navigation*. Mechanicsburg: Stackpole Books, 2005.

Wilkerson, James A., Ed. *Medicine For Mountaineering*, 3rd Edition. Seattle: The Mountaineers Books, 1985.

Yorath, C. J. *How Old is That Mountain: A Visitor's Guide to the Geology of Banff and Yoho National Parks*. Victoria: Orca Book Publishers, 1997.

TOM MORIN has scrambled extensively in the Canadian Rockies. From the beginning, he took his pastime seriously, taking courses from certified mountain guides, studying techniques for safe mountain travel and progressing at a measured pace from easy to more difficult scrambles. This book reflects the experience he gained in making the transition from hiker to scrambler.